RAISING MONEY FOR WOMEN
A Survivors' Guide

*Written for NCVO's Women's Organisations Interest Group by
Marion Bowman and Michael Norton*

*Published in association with
Directory of Social Change by
Bedford Square Press / NCVO*

Published by
BEDFORD SQUARE PRESS of the
National Council for Voluntary
Organisations
26 Bedford Square, London WC1B 3HU

© NCVO 1986

All rights reserved. No part of this
publication may be reproduced or
transmitted, in any form or by any means,
electronic, mechanical, photocopying,
recording or otherwise without the prior
permission of the publisher.

ISBN 0 7199 1170 2

First published 1986

Typeset by
D. P. Media Limited, Hitchin,
Hertfordshire

Printed and bound in England by
Henry Ling Ltd, The Dorset Press,
Dorchester, Dorset

Contents

Foreword 4

Acknowledgements 8

Part I BACKGROUND TO THE PROBLEM

1 Introduction 10
Historical background 11
New problems and new
   women's organisations 14
Voluntary sector finance 16

2 The Funding Crisis 19
Abolition of the GLC 19
Other aspects of the crisis 23
NCVO national survey 23

Part II HOW TO GO ABOUT RAISING MONEY

3 Before You Start 32
Develop clear objectives 33
Build your confidence 33
Timescales 34
How much do you need? 34
Budgeting for projects 36
Who does what? 37
Build your contacts 38
Charitable status 39
Developing a strategy and
   spending money to make
   money 40
Hints on how to ask for
   money 42
Maintaining morale and good
   public relations 43

4 The Major Statutory Sources of Funding 45
Local government 45
Central government 52
Quangos 55
Manpower Services
   Commission 60
Urban Programme 63
European Economic
   Community 65

5 The Major Non-Statutory Sources of Funding 68
Grant-making trusts 68
Companies 72
Other ways of raising money 76

6 Developing Other Sources of Funding 88
Networking 88
Who to approach 90
What to ask for 97

7 Applying for Funding and Following Up 100
Presenting your case 100
Following up 103

Part III LOOKING AHEAD

8 Strategies for Change 109
The case for women 110
Some proposals 111

Appendices
1 Sources of Further
   Information 116
2 Details from NCVO Survey
   on Funding for Women's
   Organisations 121

References 123
Index 124

Foreword

This book had its immediate roots in a meeting of the Women's Organisations Interest Group at NCVO in February 1985. The main subject was the funding of women's organisations, and speaker after speaker outlined their concern about an increasingly hostile climate in which they and others were trying to raise money for women. They also expressed despair at the enormous amount of time needed, for instance, to wade through the 2,500 plus entries in the *Directory of Grant-Making Trusts* to find out which, if any, might be sympathetic to an approach from a woman's group. With time at such a premium for most women, what was urgently needed – and currently lacking – was practical help and advice on how to find a way through the maze of different sources of statutory and non-statutory funding; an opportunity to learn from the experience of how other women's groups had managed to survive; and strategies for campaigning for better provision in the future.

The Women's Organisations Interest Group was not, of course, the first forum in which these worries had been expressed. The desperate concern of London groups, facing the imminent abolition of the GLC, had been graphically expressed during the previous month at the conference on funding for women's groups described in chapter 2. The report which Marion Bowman wrote for the Equal Opportunities Commission in 1981 on charitable funding for voluntary groups had also shown how particularly difficult it was for women's organisations to find money; other organisations like the Kentish Town Women's Workshop had started to make approaches to trusts about their policies on funding women's groups. But, symptomatic of the whole problem, there had never been the time and resources to carry through and build on these valuable initiatives.

It seemed, therefore, to the newly resuscitated Women's Organisations Interest Group, that the most urgent and useful task it could do was to respond to these concerns with *action*. Accordingly, it set up a research group into funding of women's organisations, with representation from its own members, the EOC, the LVSC and others who had done work in this field. It compiled and distributed a questionnaire on funding of women's groups, which was eventually completed by 125 organisations (see appendix 2). Most important of all, it planned this book and tried to maximise its usefulness by ensuring that the publication date was as close as possible to the abolition of the GLC and metropolitan counties on 31 March 1986 (the likely effects of which were only too apparent from the questionnaires).

We have been immensely fortunate to have found two authors who were not only able to meet our requirements – and the deadline – so successfully but who also were able to work so closely with us as a group, so patiently and with such good humour. As a result, we feel very strongly that this book speaks for us and we hope you will feel it speaks for *you*. Above all, we hope it will be truly useful and that each copy will be read as often in its published form as it was in manuscript.

We do not see it as an end in itself. As the final chapter of this book points out, there is a great need for work to be done to change the whole climate for making money available for women. Women's organisations have, on the whole, been badly served by the media. Where there is not unwarranted hostility and suspicion, there is a great ignorance of the enormous range of work that is carried out by women through such voluntary organisations. A full history of women's voluntary activity has yet to be written although chapter 1 of this book gives an outline. But one is struck by both the scale, range and variety of such work. Amongst our own members we find larger and longer established organisations like the National Federation of Women's Institutes (with approximately 350,000 members in 9,241 branches, employing 71 branch secretaries of

5

county federations and around 50 staff at headquarters), and the Women's Gas Federation and Young Homemakers (who filled Westminster Abbey for their fiftieth anniversary celebrations in May 1985), alongside newer organisations like DAWN (Drugs, Alcohol, Women Nationally), which, with only two paid workers, offers a unique information and advice service to women on all drug-related problems, and Rights of Women, a pressure group which, with a membership of 300 and a staff of 4½, gives information and legal advice on issues affecting women.

The work of many others is described in this book and the questionnaire and other contacts reveal a whole network of vigorous organisations nationwide, with pre-school playgroups in almost every suburb or village and rape crisis lines and women's aid centres in most major cities. Many locally-based groups have an influence far beyond their locality: the East London Black Women's Organisation (ELBWO) based in Newham is one example and the Hysterectomy Support Group in Lewisham another. The latter answered more than 1,500 enquiries from women all over the country in the period of January to November 1985, as they themselves said (in words that have been echoed by hundreds of groups): 'not bad for spare time,

unpaid, unfunded workers'. In the mid-1980s, when so many sectors of society are forced to depend on such workers for vital support, it is imperative to try and ensure proper recognition, which includes adequate and appropriate financial support.

Funding, as the authors of this book point out, comes from a wide range of sources and in order to change the attitudes of donors, work is needed on a number of different fronts. The male-dominated nature of the world of charitable giving has become almost a cliché. The fact that the next (1987) edition of the *Directory of Grant-Making Trusts* will have a separate category for women is a step in the right direction, but there is a whole exercise in 'consciousness-raising' on both sides to be undertaken here. In the world of corporate giving, we hope to alert companies – particularly those who employ large numbers of women – to the importance of the work of women's organisations and what they may have to offer industry.

Relevant government departments also need to be persuaded to make far more money available for women from statutory sources. Paragraph 126 of *Forward Looking Strategies for the Advancement of Women* (adopted by all participating governments – including our own – at the conference to mark the end of the

UN Decade for Women in July 1985) states: 'Governments should stimulate the formation and growth of women's organisations and women's groups and give financial and organisational support to their activities when appropriate.' We hope the implementation of these strategies will lead to a new era in governmental support for such women's organisations. Certainly it is hard to see how many will survive without it. At the same time, though, women need to explore every avenue which will lead them towards increasing their independence by raising their own money.

This book is both a practical guide and a call for action to which all are urged to respond.

Alice Burns, Chairwoman
Jane Grant, Co-ordinator
NCVO Women's Organisations Interest Group

Note:
The information in this book is relevant to women's groups in England. While it has not been possible to give detailed guidance for groups in Scotland, Wales and N. Ireland, sources of further information for these groups have been given.

Acknowledgements

The authors would like to thank the following organisations and individuals who gave invaluable help and support during the writing of this book: Jane Grant and Jo Gordon at NCVO; members of the NCVO Women's Organisations Interest Group and Alice Burns, its chairwoman; Richard Belfield, Christine Collins, Anne O'Sullivan, Irene Paul and Ama Gueye; the Equal Opportunities Commission Voluntary Organisations Unit and Information Centre; the women of the Feminist Library, Pankhurst Trust, National Child Care Campaign, Peterborough Rape Crisis Line and East London Black Women's Organisation; and Jacqueline Sallon, Editor of Bedford Square Press.

Grateful acknowledgement is made to Virginia Woolf's estate and to the Hogarth Press for permission to reproduce a quotation from *Three Guineas*.

Because of the present funding difficulties facing the voluntary sector and the particular difficulties women's organisations and ethnic minority projects have in attracting funds, the Commission for Racial Equality (CRE) is producing a fund-raising handbook for ethnic minority projects which will be published at about the same time as this book appears in print. Some of the material in this book has been adapted from material contained in the CRE's handbook. The authors of this book and the National Council for Voluntary Organisations would like to acknowledge the co-operation of the CRE in publishing this book.

PART I

BACKGROUND TO THE PROBLEM

1 Introduction

This book aims to be of some practical help to voluntary organisations run by and for women who are struggling to find the money they need to stay in existence or to get off the ground.

The term 'voluntary organisation' is interpreted broadly to mean a self-governing body of people who are working voluntarily to improve a particular aspect of life. It is a non-statutory group set up through the motivation of the participants themselves. An organisation or group of this type may or may not employ full-time or part-time staff, but they will almost always be dependent to a greater or lesser extent on funds which they raise from a variety of external sources. Organisations and groups which are inspired by the particular needs and interests of women, which are very diverse, often appear to find fund raising more frustrating than many other special interest groups, such as those concerned with children, elderly people, or even animals (see chapter 2).

The reason for this is bound up with the status of women in society. Despite the fact that there is a Queen on the throne and a woman in 10 Downing Street, women as a group wield little power, whether financial or political. Women have less money than men to use in support of voluntary activity. Women have less influence than men in deciding how money, in the form of grants, should be allocated. Women's needs are not adequately met by official or statutory agencies. Women therefore organise in self-governing voluntary groups to try to meet those needs themselves. Persuading others to support women's voluntary action financially has always been a problem precisely because of prevailing attitudes about women's role: their prime responsibility is seen to be the care of their own families in their own homes. The very fact that women do join together in groups and organisations has often been regarded as a threat. Starving women of finance and resources like meeting places is only one of the responses women have had from their opponents. Ridicule and suppression are also familiar tactics.

This book is therefore both a handbook on how to find funds and a campaigning book in support of women's claim, not just to patronage, but to power itself. Information can help women's groups survive immediate funding crises like the abolition of the Greater London Council and the metropolitan county councils. So we detail the range of funding bodies – both statutory and non-statutory – to whom women might consider applying. We also suggest ways in which women might be able to develop the resources at their own disposal through networking, co-operation and mutual support.

But in the longer term, women's groups can only be adequately funded if the prevailing policies of the funding world change in women's favour, and ultimately if women's own powers of patronage are enhanced by the achievement of true equality. With this in mind we also offer some suggestions for change, for further debate and action.

HISTORICAL BACKGROUND

The connections between women's status in a male-dominated society, their organising in voluntary groups and the problems they have with financing the work needed to alleviate suffering or bring about change have a long history. Despite the fact that the state first acknowledged its responsibility for conditions in society with the Poor Law of 1601, it remained largely a matter for voluntary action. The upheavals in both urban and rural life during the nineteenth century spurred 'philanthropy' on to new dimensions and significance and women were central participants as donors, volunteers and recipients (F. K. Prochaska, 1980).

During the 1800s, huge amounts of money were circulating in charitable circles. It has been

Background to the Problem

estimated that middle-class households gave around 10 per cent of their income away to charity, and in 1885, *The Times* reported that charitable receipts in London alone came to more than the national budgets of Denmark, Sweden or Portugal.

Until the rise of women's trade unions, themselves voluntary organisations, the charity of working-class women was undocumented. But the generosity of the poor towards the poor was extensive whether through providing food for families with no income, looking after neighbours' children, helping out during sickness or whip-rounds in pubs at times of crisis. Written records show the extent of women's involvement in institutional forms of philanthropy. The first major call on women's contributions, organisational talent and fund-raising ingenuity came from the Bible and missionary societies in the early part of the century. Women's 'auxiliaries' were formed and although they were the most successful fund raisers, they were excluded from exercising any control over the management of the societies. Their very involvement elicited considerable opposition, especially from churchmen themselves. One, quoted by Prochaska, expressed his misgivings in terms which were to be echoed over and over again whenever women grouped together. He warned of 'vain and unfeminine women, feverish for publicity who neglect their domestic duties', of 'women too stupid to administer efficiently or even add up their collections correctly', of 'amazonian women who challenge attention and put us on our defence' (page 25).

The records also show that from the start, women began to support organisations relevant to women's own needs. There were groups such as the Institution for the Employment of Needlewomen, the Women's Protective and Provident League, and the Southwark Female Society for the Relief of Sickness and Extreme Want. The charitable work women became involved in, such as prison and workhouse visiting and rescue missions, developed into campaigns for legal and social reform not simply on humanitarian issues but also on issues reflecting the status of women in society. For many women, organised voluntary charity work was a profession in a world where other doors were closed. It gave them experience of government, law, education, administration, medicine and social service, and voluntary organisation itself became the tool by which women began to force those closed doors open. Women trained in charitable societies were prominent among those who petitioned the House of Commons for female suffrage in 1866 and who formed the National Society for Women's Suffrage in 1867. Some women's voluntary organisations grew out of broader movements such as the Women's Co-operative Guild, founded in 1884. Others, such as the Women's Social and Political Union, developed as a result of the increasing unwillingness of women to rely on mixed organisations (that is, organisations with women as members but which are controlled by men) to make justice for women a priority.

The story of the WSPU is an example of why women's status itself is sufficient stimulus to the formation of autonomous women's organisations which make their own needs their sole priority. It was formed in Manchester in 1903 by women members of the Independent Labour Party (ILP) annoyed to discover that a meeting hall whose construction they had contributed to was being used by a branch of the party which did not accept women as members.

The financial history of the WSPU is also of interest. To begin with they were unable to be completely self-financing. Male patronage was crucial. To cover the cost of speakers being sent all over the north of England, the WSPU was mainly dependent on the ILP. They had no funds to cover the hire of Caxton Hall in London in 1906 when they organised the first of many Women's Marches to Parliament, so Keir Hardie, their most prominent male supporter, persuaded two friends to make a loan of £50. It was publicity stunts such as the Women's March and, soon after, the first imprisonments, which helped the WSPU to grow, increasing controversy over their aims and tactics but also increasing their support. Much of it now came from wealthy individuals, notably Emmeline and Fred Pethick-Lawrence who were both well connected and served as treasurers for the organisation.

By 1907, the WSPU had expanded to 47 branches with nine paid organisers. Income totalled £2,959 and expenditure was £2,494. By June 1908, the WSPU was able to finance what still in 1985 remained the largest rally ever seen in London when 500,000 people gathered in Hyde Park. Thirty special trains brought people to London from 70 different cities, seven processions converged on 20 platforms in the Park, thousands of flags were made as well as 700 purple, green and white banners, each 8 feet by 3 feet, and a huge advertising campaign was mounted with enormous posters in shops and on buses and a barge sailing past the House of Commons inviting Members of Parliament to take part (Andrew Rosen, 1974).

NEW PROBLEMS AND NEW WOMEN'S ORGANISATIONS

Few women's causes nowadays have the same attraction for modern-day philanthropists or benefactors, or for mass support, as the WSPU. Indeed many might expect less need for women's causes with the vote secured and the welfare state offering a safety net against the worst effects of poverty and sickness. But as society has changed so have women's needs and the second half of the twentieth century has seen women's voluntary organisations enter a new phase of growth and vitality. This vitality has not grown out of the strength of funding for women's projects, but from the commitment and contribution of women themselves. The more traditional women's organisations whose roots are in the suffrage period, such as the National Union of Townswomen's Guilds, the National Federation of Women's Institutes, or the Soroptimist International of Great Britain and Ireland, have been joined by newer groups which have emerged in response to the changing patterns of British life. There have been increases in the numbers of elderly people, of single-parent families, of working mothers; the problems of racism, of discrimination against women in work or of the exclusion of people with disabilities from all areas of life are unrelenting. Cuts in government spending on welfare, social and health services have also meant a revival of fund raising for traditional charitable causes such as supplying equipment for hospitals and schools. Changes in government policy affecting matters such as the care of elderly or sick people in the community rather than in institutions have revived traditional expectations that women will be available to shoulder much of the burden unpaid in the home.

Women have been the first to feel the effects of these changes in society so it is not surprising to find that women have responded to them by organising together, to provide services and to act as pressure groups. Contemporary concerns have been identified and new ways of working have been developed. Women's aid refuges, rape crisis lines, lesbian links, vocational support and training groups like Women in Housing, have all developed in a climate of renewed feminist activity. Women's voluntary organisations now range over issues which arise specifically from gender, such as health matters; from the position of women in society, such as childcare needs; and from the purely feminist aspirations of women to organise as women, such as cultural enterprises. The emergence of black women's groups highlights the motivation of all women to win a measure of self-determination in a society which prescribes limited, stereotyped roles for women.

Black women have taken action to establish services, pressure groups and support networks for themselves in order to counteract the racism of white-dominated women's groups. This development is a close echo of the resistance to subordination and discrimination which has consistently driven women of all colours to organise separately from men. But black women have also stressed that racism in the wider society means they do not always see their activities in isolation from men. Their political perspectives are different from those of white women and so their objectives and the manner in which they organise to work for solutions also often differ. Self-determination means different things to different women.

The renewed vigour of women's voluntary action is evidence of the continuing relevance of women's organisations. It is an important component in the overall growth of voluntary organisations in recent decades. It has been estimated that between 1960 and 1970, the number of voluntary organisations almost doubled. It is difficult to get an accurate picture as no systematic monitoring or research is done. Assessing the scale of groups operating at a local level is even more difficult. Little monitoring is done and by their nature local groups are self-motivating and often feel no obligation to account for themselves to a third party. NCVO does recognise the special interests of women as a group and women's issues have begun to play a more important role in NCVO's work. The Women's Organisations Interest Group of NCVO national member organisations was revived in 1984 (see Foreword), and greater priority is now being given to promoting women's issues in the voluntary sector.

Other bodies, both statutory and non-statutory, also keep close contact with women's voluntary organisations. The Voluntary Services Unit at the Home Office has an important liaison role in the development of government policy towards the voluntary sector, but it has no special brief on women's organisations. The Equal Opportunities Commission, however, has a special unit working in this area, and the Women's National Commission, an advisory committee to the government, is a communication link between statutory and voluntary sectors. It was formed in 1969 to ensure that women's opinions were given due weight in the deliberations of Government. Other purely voluntary associations and federations, such as the Standing Conference of

Women's Organisations, the Women's Aid Federation, or the Community Roots Trust, also maintain links with a wide network of groups. The Councils for Voluntary Service – National Association (CVSNA) is developing its work with women's organisations too.

VOLUNTARY SECTOR FINANCE

In common with the nineteenth century, huge amounts of money still circulate in the voluntary sector, which is by no means limited to registered charities. Gifts to the top 200 charities alone in 1984/85 amounted to almost £1,000 million, with the league leaders themselves receiving several millions of pounds each, as the table below shows:

Voluntary Income of Top Ten Charities

		£000
1	Oxfam	25,550
2	National Trust	24,666
3	Royal National Lifeboat Institution	20,995
4	Cancer Research Campaign	20,089
5	Imperial Cancer Research Fund	17,815
6	Salvation Army	17,073
7	Dr Barnardo's	16,912
8	Save the Children Fund	12,007
9	NSPCC	11,743
10	Help the Aged	11,537

Note:
These figures cover gifts and subscriptions, not sales revenue or central and local government grants.

Source:
Charity Statistics 1984/85, Charities Aid Foundation

Special interest groups of all types are catered for by the charities which feature in the Charities Aid Foundation's list of the top 200 grant-seeking charities. As well as those featured above, that is, the starving, lovers of the national heritage and landscape, seafarers, cancer sufferers, the homeless and destitute, children and elderly people, the list includes blind people, animals, birds, the sick, wildlife, scouts, donkeys, arts lovers and many more. The first ostensibly 'women's' organisation to be listed is the Girl Guides Association at number 91. The only other charity of direct benefit to women to make the top 200 is the Royal Masonic Institution for Girls at 106.

These figures reveal the great generosity of the British public when called upon to give to charity, although it is the traditional 'good cause' charities which benefit the most.

Crises like the Ethiopian famine and earthquake or volcanic

disasters appear to increase the total amount given to charitable causes rather than divert money from domestic to overseas concerns.

Much has been made by the present government of the need for voluntary activity to be financed by sources other than the state, and yet the most significant development in recent years has not so much been the retreat of government from voluntary sector finance as the increase in central government and quango grants over local government grants. The implications for voluntary sector funding of the abolition of the Greater London Council and the metropolitan county councils can be seen as part of this overall trend. In 1983/84, cash payments from local authorities were, at £351 million, nearly twice those of central government. Fees for voluntary organisations' services purchased by local authorities accounted for about 40 per cent of that sum and rate relief given to charities accounted for about a third.

However, central government has increased its share of finance to the voluntary sector from about a fifth of total central and local government expenditure in 1978 to more than a third. What is more, the combination of central government and quango grants now dwarfs local government grant giving, according to *Charity Statistics*. Of particular note is the increasing importance of the Manpower Services Commission in providing support. In 1984, the voluntary sector received as much as £285,300,000 through the various programmes for the unemployed. One of the implications of the trend is the centralisation of decision making, and the limited accessibility and accountability of central government and quangos, which are unelected, compared with local government. At the same time there is increasingly close scrutiny by grant-makers of the groups which receive grants. This can have a seriously adverse effect on innovative, radical or new voluntary organisations which do not have conventional structures or philosophies. Women's groups, in particular, which are noted for pioneering voluntary action, stand to suffer the most.

In addition to government, the other major institutional sources of finance for the voluntary sector are charitable trusts and companies. In 1984/85, the total amount donated by the 200 most generous companies was £43 million, a figure far outstripped by the £223 million given away by the top 200 grant-making trusts.

What women's share was of this considerable fortune in finance for voluntary and charitable causes is unknown. What is known is that women experience great difficulty in persuading donors to support their organisations and projects. Accurate monitoring is impossible unless there is an explicit policy to measure developments against and few grant-makers have clear policies. Some which do have policies are reluctant to make them public. Others may have policies which they make public but these will almost certainly not be concerned with the needs of women. The Labour-controlled Greater London Council, now abolished, was the most significant of the handful of grant-making bodies with publicly known policies which recognised the needs of women. In its final year the Women's Committee of the GLC approved nearly £10 million in grant aid to voluntary groups in London. During the same period, the grant aid budget of the Equal Opportunities Commission, which has national responsibilities, was a mere £71,000.

The history of women's organisations reveals their determination to identify their own needs, and to devote their time, money and effort to meeting them. But demands for the recognition and support of the community and nation at large are also part of that history. What women want now is a more equitable share of the national fortune which ensures a vigorous, conscientious and richly varied voluntary sector.

2
The Funding Crisis

ABOLITION OF THE GLC

On 13 January 1985, women from over 80 organisations gathered at Camden Town Hall in London to discuss the funding crisis likely to be precipitated by abolition of the Greater London Council. The six morning workshops on that day reflected the major concerns of a significant proportion of the women's voluntary sector, not just in London but throughout the country: the needs of black and ethnic minority women, childcare, the establishment of women's centres, training and employment, health and housing.

Soon afterwards, an open letter was sent to all women members of the Houses of Commons and Lords from London women's groups concerned about the effects the Local Government Bill would have on women in London if it was passed. It was a clear and concise description of the serious implications abolition would have for women's voluntary activity, so we quote it here in full:

Although women make up 52 per cent of the population we are clearly a disadvantaged group.[Statistics showing the inequalities women face in jobs, pay, training and family responsibilities were included in an appendix.] As you know, local authorities have no statutory duty to challenge discrimination on grounds of

sex, promote our interests or create opportunities for us. However, over recent years the GLC has taken a lead in developing overall policies aimed at achieving those ends. This has included the development of equal opportunities policies for both GLC employees and employees of groups grant-aided by the GLC, and the systematic consideration of women's needs and interests in the services and facilities provided in London. As the Bill contains no provision for the continuation of this strategic work, we can only assume that it will cease, to the great detriment of women's interests in London.

Another important development has been the provision of grant aid to women's groups and projects which has enabled us to express our own needs and find our own ways of meeting them. The Women's Committee of the GLC has itself approved more than £9½ million in grant aid for the current financial year. This has provided funding for more than 400 groups run by and for women. These include:

- 187 grants to childcare and youth projects
- 74 grants to women's centres, which provide a range of support, advice, education and childcare services, as well as space for women to meet together
- numerous projects which provide training for women in traditionally male areas of work such as building and motor mechanics
- design and architecture projects which look at building design with women's needs in mind
- women's aid refuges, which provide safe shelter for battered women
- black and ethnic minority women's groups, health groups, groups for older women, girls' projects, lesbian groups, groups for women with disabilities

The range is vast. We are obviously concerned, as we hope you will be, that this range of services should not be lost as this would cause suffering to the women who currently use the services, the women currently employed in them and the women who would be forced, once again, to take on the unpaid caring role.

The proposals contained in Clause 46 of the Bill are cumbersome and insufficient to maintain the current level of funding to the voluntary sector in general, and to women's groups in particular. They have done nothing to allay our fears, especially as they refer only to London-wide groups, whereas one of the strengths of women's groups is that they tend to be very locally based.

The other option proposed is that of turning to the local authority for grant aid. But history has shown that this is usually not an alternative for women's groups. Very few local authorities have supported women's activities. Indeed, a number have been known to throw every possible obstacle in the paths of women's groups which have received funding from elsewhere, so deep is their opposition to the idea of women organising for themselves. It is this kind of attitude which has led many groups to turn to the GLC for their first opportunity to create innovative projects providing services when and where they are needed.

Grant aid has been particularly important for black and ethnic minority women, who experience double discrimination. Again the GLC has taken a lead in this area by making it a priority through its grant-aiding and policy work to tackle this discrimination and to respond to the needs of black and ethnic minority women. Thus black and ethnic minority women have been given the resources they need to come together and tackle their own needs in their own way. It is vital that this work is enabled to continue.

The Government has made a commitment to protect 'worthwhile' voluntary groups, but it is well known that in the Government's view, women's groups often do not fall into this category despite the valuable work we do and the services we provide. As women, we are sure you share many of our concerns about the future. The Local Government Bill does not even mention women and we feel that once again our needs are being ignored and the progress we have made is being undermined. We would therefore urge you to bear women's interests in mind during the debates on the Bill and to oppose any measures which are detrimental to us.

The immediate result of this letter was that two women peers, Lady Ewart-Biggs and Lady Vickers, met with some of the women's groups in London. Lady Ewart-Biggs was taken in the Stockwell Women's Lift Service to visit the Dalston Children's Centre in its new premises. She and Lady Vickers then met women from Croydon Women's Centre, Haringey Women's Education and Training, Migrant Service Unit, London Community Health Resource, Sutton Women's Centre and the National Council for One-Parent Families. It was a useful exchange, but women's worst fears became reality when the abolition Bill became law with

Background to the Problem

Royal Assent on 15 July 1985. The Greater London Council ceased to exist on 31 March 1986 along with the six English metropolitan county councils – Greater Manchester, Merseyside, Tyne and Wear, West Yorkshire, South Yorkshire and West Midlands. The grant-making role of the metropolitan counties had been less prominent than that of the GLC, but the removal of this complete tier of local government has serious implications for future grant aid for women's activities.

The voluntary sector as a whole won some important concessions from the government and the arrangements made for grant aid after abolition are detailed in chapter 4 (see page 49). But the failure of the campaign to save the GLC and the metropolitan county councils immediately plunged a wide range of voluntary groups into a state of crisis. The funding arrangements made for the organisations previously supported by the seven authorities were condemned as inadequate. The total amount of money available is considerably less and there are no provisions for developmental work to help disadvantaged groups maximise their call on funds. It is inevitable that some will not survive. The district and borough councils are expected to take up part of the funding role of the GLC and metropolitan counties. But the policies of some London boroughs, particularly Barnet, Bromley and Westminster, indicate that the collapse of some voluntary groups is a deliberately-sought consequence of the GLC's demise. The general confusion and lack of a united political will in the county-wide structures can only serve to make matters worse.

GLC funding in particular has had a major impact on the expectations, development and dependency of a number of women's organisations. For the first time ever substantial sums of money have been made available for women's projects which have thrived in a multitude of forms. Women, used to being short of money, have developed greater expertise and professionalism. More paid jobs have been created, at better rates of pay, and have been filled through the application of equal opportunities policies. (Incidentally, the voluntary sector employs many more women than men, with an average salary of only £5,850 nett, a reflection of the fact that women continue to be a pool of cheap labour in the economy as a whole.) The efficiency and reliability of the services offered has increased. Women's expectations of adequate funding have been raised and they will be unwilling to lower them again. But the fact that many have been almost entirely funded by the GLC is the saddest irony. For them, the crisis is all the more severe. Later in this chapter we look at some case studies of groups funded by the GLC, and of other groups struggling to find funds.

OTHER ASPECTS OF THE CRISIS

Other factors have also contributed to funding problems. Cuts in the Urban Programme, the major vehicle for central government grant aid (see page 63), have both reduced the availability of money and removed eligibility from certain areas. Women's Aid Refuges, which offer women and children a safe haven from domestic violence, and Rape Crisis Lines, which help women survive sexual assault, have received crucial support through the Urban Programme, and cuts will be a serious threat to this work in some areas. It is not uncommon already for Women's Aid groups to help women escaping from violent partners by putting them up in members' homes. Rate capping has left the voluntary sector vulnerable when local authorities have looked at discretionary funding as an area where savings could be made. And on top of that, local authorities have been cutting their own 'caring' services, such as home helps, day care and meals on wheels, putting further pressure on women as both consumers and carers. Indeed, it is the policy of central government to push the responsibility for the care of vulnerable groups back into the community. On the whole, in this context 'community' is synonymous with 'women'.

Elsewhere, the European Social Fund, which has made special provision for women (see page 65) has adopted new guidelines making it more difficult for women in Britain to win support. Amongst non-statutory donors, companies have been accused of 'meanness' by Michael Brophy, director of the Charities Aid Foundation. Companies' gifts to charity were not increasing in line with their profits, CAF's *Charity Statistics 1984/85* revealed. Profits of some of the largest firms had risen by an average of 31 per cent while their total gifts to charities rose by only 19 per cent in the same period.

NCVO NATIONAL SURVEY

The Women's Organisations Interest Group at NCVO decided to survey women's organisations to get a measure of the range of women's voluntary work, their financial needs and their fund-raising problems. The full analysis of the survey can be found in appendix 2 but we include the most significant points here.

The survey was by no means fully comprehensive. One hundred

and twenty national organisations received questionnaires and an unknown number of local groups were sent questionnaires through the councils for voluntary service around the UK. Locally-based London groups are under-represented in the results which were analysed from 125 completed questionnaires by Jo Gordon at NCVO.

The main feature to emerge from the sample is the diversity of issues which women identify as priorities. One hundred and five organisations said that 'women' were the main focus of their work, but they gave more detail of how they define women's concerns than this blanket category might indicate. From this it is clear that 'women's interests' (taken to mean the matters affecting women's lives) are wide-ranging and far from uniform. They include childcare, the family, equality of parental responsibility, housing, youth work with girls, sexual abuse, rape, social and domestic violence, abortion, anti-racist work, legal and welfare advice, education, research and training. The majority of groups have memberships ranging from 10 to 500. A few have memberships running to several thousands. Most combine paid staff and volunteers and annual budgets range from less than £50 to over £1 million. Eighteen of the 125 had been formed since April 1984.

The questions on funding showed that local government was the most important source of support, although less than half were funded in this way. Only 10 received grants from central government departments. Thirteen received Urban Programme support. Twenty-six organisations received small amounts (£50–£200) from trusts and other grant-making bodies. As might be expected from its meagre budget, the Equal Opportunities Commission was negligible as a funding body (see page 55). Only 15 relied on membership subscriptions bringing in at least 50 per cent of their income and a handful had received small donations in cash and kind from industry, commerce and trade unions. Widespread fund-raising activities like bazaars, coffee mornings, jumble sales and market stalls supplemented grants, as did sales of goods and services. Only a very few relied totally on their own resources or those of a parent body, and did not seek funds from elsewhere.

But it was the written comments rather than the statistical information which were the most revealing. The key issue of concern to groups was the reluctance of funding bodies to recognise the special needs of women and the seriousness of some of the problems facing them. All other problems seemed to flow from that underlying prejudice. Black women faced the additional problem of racism. The fact that some groups were all-female actually annoyed some funding bodies. Projects initiated by women were seen as unpopular, controversial or 'political' despite the absence of any party political affiliation. The other major concerns were:

- the difficulties campaigning groups face when trying to register as charities
- increasing bureaucracy delaying payment of grants with a resultant increase in costs
- uncertainty about continuation of grants
- 'cliff-hanging' lateness of confirmation of grants
- the bleak outlook for new organisations in the light of inadequate finance for existing groups
- lack of publicity and sexist media coverage preventing the dissemination of information which might stimulate increased membership
- need always outstripping provision
- the inability to expand by moving to larger premises or employing more staff
- the difficulty in finding funds for general overheads, particularly staff, rather than special projects

Throughout, organisations and groups mentioned lack of time, money and information as barriers to successful fund raising. Basic resources such as these are usually met by members themselves. But women's time is a precious commodity. Housework, childcare, caring for sick or elderly family members, and paid employment all eat into the time women can devote to their own interests. And one survey respondent noted: 'Since most women have either no personal income or are earners because it is necessary to supplement family income, they often find it difficult to subscribe to organisations.'

Some of these problems – and, it should be said, the success with which women can sometimes meet the challenge of fund raising – are highlighted in the case studies we feature here.

Feminist Library and Information Centre (formerly *Women's Research and Resources Centre*)
Hungerford House
Victoria Embankment
London WC2N 6PA
Tel: 01-930 0715

Feminist Library, a registered charity, was founded in 1975 and is a large and ever-growing collection of books, pamphlets, periodicals and unpublished papers from the post-1968 Women's Liberation Movement. It is housed in GLC-owned premises at a peppercorn rent and is open to all, free. Annual membership subscriptions (to borrow) range from £1 (for unemployed people) to £12 (for institutions), but income from this source and others, e.g. sales, is negligible in relation to costs, currently around £50,000 a year. The major expense is salaries for four workers on a four-day week.

They point out that no public library is self-financing and the Feminist Library, which is heavily used as a London-wide service, has to be subsidised to survive. Since 1981 it has been almost completely subsidised by the GLC. Abolition has left the library vulnerable to closure because of the uncertainty of other potential funding sources which have been identified as the London Grant Unit (known as the Richmond Scheme), the Inner London Education Authority, some London boroughs and some charitable trusts. The EOC and charitable trusts have funded them in the past. Specific problems are lack of sympathy with an explicitly feminist service, the time-consuming effort of perpetual need to make grant applications and the preference of funders for supporting specific projects rather than general work of the organisation.

East London Black Women's Organisation
745 Barking Road
London E13 9ER
Tel: 01-552 1169

The East London Black Women's Organisation was set up in 1979 because of a strong commitment by a group of African/Caribbean women who, among other aims, wished to re-establish the rights of black women to meet together as people of African descent. The organisation developed originally, like so many black women's groups, out of concern with issues like the difficulties black children face in the education system. Later the organisation widened its scope to include welfare rights, counselling sessions on childcare, health, nationality, cultural activities and the building up of an information resource base in order to cater for the unmet needs of black women in the area.

The organisation operates as a collective which is open to black women who share its objectives. The group also has men as associate members who are invited to specific meetings. The management committee is elected at annual general meetings from the general, full membership. Charitable status is pending and ELBWO is to become a limited company.

After operating for several years on a purely voluntary basis, the group applied in 1983 to the GLC Women's Committee for funding for a black women's centre. A grant of £56,000 covered the salaries of four full-time workers and other costs such as rent, rates, office equipment, etc. Other smaller sums have been granted by the London Borough of Newham and the Arts Council for specific projects. Several unsuccessful applications to the Urban Programme have been made with the aim of securing funds to purchase a building to give ELBWO a permanent home. ELBWO's problems are compounded by limited employment prospects in East London, bad housing, low educational achievement and the pressure of racism.

Pankhurst Trust
c/o 39 Egerton Road North
Manchester M21 1SN
Tel: 061-225 3895

The Pankhurst Trust, a registered charity, is renovating Emmeline Pankhurst's home in Manchester, a listed building, as an exhibition centre devoted to women's suffrage and a resource centre for women's voluntary groups with a crèche, café, office space, meeting rooms, workshop, information service and reprographic facilities. Fund raising for Phases 1 and 2 (of three) of the building work has been successful with substantial grants totalling £215,000 from the Urban Programme, Historic Buildings Council, Greater Manchester Council and the Granada Foundation, and smaller amounts totalling £20,000 from members of the public, companies and charitable trusts. Labour costs are being met through the Manpower Services Commission Community Programme.

Administrative costs have been met by grants from the EOC, Manchester City Council and individual donations. Other income is generated through covenants, gifts in kind, and fund-raising/promotional activity which has included sponsored walks, a Friends group, cake raffles, the annual Sylvia Pankhurst Memorial Lecture, street collections, a drama production, and sales of the Manchester Women's History Walk and annual year planner.

Further fund-raising effort is needed to build Phase 3, to prepare the permanent suffrage exhibition, and to equip the crèche, café, administrative office and information centre.

The trust estimates that a minimum of £40,000 per annum is needed to staff, maintain and run the centre in the first year of opening (1987). Income generated from membership subscriptions, café profit, bookstall sales, and charges for the use of facilities, is expected to be around £12,000, leaving £28,000 to be found from other sources. The trust will apply to central and local government and charitable trusts.

Background to the Problem

National Childcare Campaign
Wesley House
70 Great Queen Street
London WC2B 5AX
Tel: 01-405 5617

The National Childcare Campaign aims to increase childcare provision. It lobbies central and local government and works with other childcare campaigns and projects throughout the country at grassroots level. It provides a range of services to member organisations and deals with queries on childcare whatever the source. Services include giving practical guidance on matters such as staff : child ratios in nurseries and advice on suitable literature for use with the under-fives. The campaign also runs workshops on topics such as good anti-racist and anti-sexist practice in childcare, the educational development of children and the integration of younger children with older children.

The NCCC was established in 1980 but 'took off' in 1982 thanks to annual funding from the GLC, which was £73,000 in 1985/86. An additional £30,000 comes from the Department of Health and Social Security and the campaign acts as an agent for four other projects, handling another £90,000 from the DHSS on their behalf. Their income has also included small amounts from charges for services and grants from the EOC and Commission for Racial Equality (CRE).

Membership stood at 300 individuals and organisations in 1985 when the NCCC launched a membership drive. Subscription rates were £7.50 (individuals), £10 (groups), and £30 (national organisations). The cost of servicing members with newsletters, minutes, annual reports, policy papers and the Annual General Meeting is subsidised by the grants. An increase in membership to around 1,000 would cover administration costs and bring an increase in sales and voluntary effort.

Several years of generous funding from the GLC has transformed the organisation which has developed beyond an amateurish approach. It is now the main organisation to which people, particularly at grass-roots level, turn for information and advice on childcare. The campaign has a strong anti-racist commitment. The loss of the GLC's core funding therefore has serious implications for the NCCC. Replacing it has proved difficult. With abolition certain they turned to the DHSS as a possible source of core funding. Other avenues for additional funds were the London Boroughs Grant Unit, trade unions, charitable trusts and educational trusts.

In an effort to survive, the NCCC is separating its servicing and campaigning function so that its service wing – the Daycare Trust – can be registered as a charity.

Peterborough Rape Crisis Line
Tel: 0773-40515

A group of 10 women founded the Peterborough Rape Crisis Line in late 1983 to offer a completely confidential service to women who have been victims of rape, sexual abuse and sexual harassment of any type. A grant of £1,200 over 10 months from Opportunities for Volunteering, a DHSS scheme, helped establish the service by paying workers and covering the cost of overheads. Since that funding ran out the group has received £50 from Cambridgeshire Social Services Committee, £15 from the National Union of Public Employees and £150 from the National Union of Journalists. This last donation has helped meet the cost of an answering machine. A request for support from Peterborough City Council brought the response that the council was not in a position to help them. The group has around £200–300 in the bank at any one time, mainly raised through fund-raising activities such as jumble sales and through personal donations.

The telephone line is answered by volunteers only twice a week – Tuesday evenings between 7.30 pm and 10 pm, and Saturday mornings between 10 am and 12 noon. Lack of funds means that the group is unable to extend its service although it aims to provide confidential counselling – by telephone or face to face – for women who have been sexually assaulted; to accompany women to police stations or to court if necessary; to give information on topics such as VD clinics, abortion, legal proceedings and likely outcome. Finance is also needed to pay for the training of volunteers, for publicity and educational work and for overheads.

The group estimates that with a full-time worker to sustain the Rape Crisis Line at an adequate level, the annual budget would be a minimum of £13,000.

PART II

HOW TO GO ABOUT RAISING MONEY

3
Before You Start

The very first thing you should do is decide how your group or organisation is going to manage its affairs. If you have been in existence for some time and are embarking on a new phase of fund raising, you should work out whether your current structure for decision making is adequate and carries the full support of everyone in the organisation.

Women's organisations can take different forms – conventional structures with trustees, a management or executive committee and paid staff, collectives made up of both paid staff and volunteers, or a combination of management, staff and users. You might be a registered friendly society or co-operative or a company limited by guarantee. You will probably be committed to democratic procedures and full consultation. However you arrange things, you will have to decide how the various roles are performed and responsibilities met to ensure efficiency and effectiveness. You are a self-governing body and self-government means self-management. Good management is invaluable, so if you keep that in mind you can't go wrong.

There is no blueprint to success at fund raising. You must do what you think will work for you on a scale which you as a group and as individuals can cope with. Don't be over-ambitious and risk the demoralisation of failure. Before you start, take the time to talk through the work you are trying to do, the group's strengths and weaknesses, and plan your moves. In this chapter we discuss some key points which we think will improve your chances of success.

DEVELOP CLEAR OBJECTIVES

Don't assume that the reason for your group's existence is obvious – even to the women involved. Whether you are a long-established organisation with a formal structure, procedures and constitution, or a newly-formed group whose formation was stimulated by an immediate set of circumstances, it's a good idea to discuss why you have all got together in the first place. Do you all share the same view on what you are trying to achieve? Are there any serious differences of opinion? If there are and they rumble on unaired and unresolved it could cause problems. It's easier to convince other people of the justice of your case if you are clear yourselves on what your case is and fully convinced of it. If not, the differences may well emerge later when it comes to spending the money you've raised, putting the success of the project in jeopardy.

BUILD YOUR CONFIDENCE

One of the main keys to success is morale. You must feel confident about your organisation and what it is doing and also about your ability to raise the money you need.

If you are helping with fund raising, you must come over as positive in the letters you write, or when you speak to people on the telephone or at meetings. If there's a woman locally who runs assertiveness training sessions, ask her if she would be willing to organise one for your group – as a donation in kind, of course! It might help dispel any nervousness or timidity amongst you. Thrash out a way of presenting yourselves and your work that you all feel comfortable with. Use your successes to boost your confidence. Learn from your failures. Don't take things personally or get dispirited too easily. Fund raising is difficult. There's a lot of competition. But don't give up. Keep telling yourself that the work you're doing is important and that the money will be found to do it eventually. Each time you ask for money be as enthusiastic and optimistic as the first time you asked, however many times you may have failed since then.

Never apologise. Never run yourselves down. Never say 'I know there are just as many worthy causes as ours' or 'I'm

33

sorry to bother you, you must be very busy.' You are just feeding people with the reasons to turn you down. Believe in your own importance and worth, and others will, too.

TIMESCALES

It is important to establish how much time you've got to achieve the results you're aiming for. Are you fund raising for something specific which has a beginning, a middle and an end, or do you need the money to keep going in a more general sense? Try to set realistic deadlines whatever the purpose of the fund raising. It gives a bit of shape and substance to what can otherwise become a rambling, never-ending struggle. Set a pace to your fund raising to keep the momentum going. Even if it's slow, if you've thought in advance of how much time it might take to achieve what you're setting out to do, your expectations will be more realistic. This is essential to keeping your spirits up. If you don't reach the target by the deadline, don't worry. Set yourself a new target and a new deadline for raising the rest of the money you need.

A common problem is leaving everything until it's too late. Try to plan your fund raising so that you never get to a point of crisis. It always takes longer to raise money than you think. It can take months or even longer to negotiate grants or to organise an effective appeal. If you need a lot of money, you should allow yourselves at least a year to plan what to do before asking anybody for anything. If you haven't that amount of time, or the amounts of money you need are relatively small, try to use fund-raising methods which don't need a lot of bureaucratic 'toing and froing' and which can bring rapid results.

HOW MUCH DO YOU NEED?

For some organisations, fund raising can become the one activity which overshadows all others, but it's important to see it as a task in itself so that the work the money's being raised for remains the focus. One way of doing this is to budget, so that the task becomes manageable. Fund raising will probably be a permanent feature of the life of most voluntary organisations, but it will be easier to keep on top of it if you identify particular amounts of money to meet specific needs.

Try to enlist the voluntary help of someone with financial skills, like a bookkeeper or accountant who could at the very least give you advice. Decide who is going to be responsible for keeping the financial records. Make friends with your bank manager and talk over the group's finances with her/him.

Work out the amount of money you will need for the coming year. Make a list of all the things you will spend money on. This may sound like putting the cart before the horse. You may feel you can't possibly make plans to spend money before you've raised it and that the best way to proceed is to meet costs as they arise and as the money comes in. For some people there may be no other way of surviving, but if you possibly can, plan. It increases your sense of control which pays off in terms of morale and operational efficiency.

Some costs can be precisely determined. Others will be estimated. Some items will be donated in kind but include them in your budget anyway so that you get the full picture. You will then have a statement of your financial requirements for doing the very important job you have set out to do, and a shopping list for soliciting donations in kind.

Your list might have headings like these (this list is not fully inclusive):

Occupancy costs

rent and rates *or* hire of meeting
    rooms
maintenance of the building
depreciation of equipment
heating and lighting
insurance
interest on mortgage or bank loan

Administration costs

wages, including national
    insurance
services such as cleaning,
    bookkeeping or accountancy
telephone
postage
stationery and photocopying
sundry expenses (travel, training,
    office equipment)

Fund-raising costs

Ironically, fund raising itself can be a very expensive business, even if all that's involved is collecting membership subscriptions or making grant applications. When you come to working out how you are going to try to raise the money you need, bear this in mind. Assess your fund-raising costs and include them in your overall budget.

Don't forget to make an adjustment for inflation. When you've estimated your costs, you need to estimate your income. If you don't already have any to speak of this is where you start planning your fund raising.

Note down the income you already have and the income which is probable. You may have a three-year grant from a charitable trust and a clear indication that your local authority will continue to support you. You may already be making plans to hold another sponsored walk or jumble sale since the last one raised, say, £500. You will also need to estimate any income from sales of goods or services such as your excellent pamphlet on women's health provision locally or that evening class you're running every year for the Workers' Educational Association on women and welfare benefits.

Deduct the total expected income from your planned expenditure and you're left with the deficit which you have to plan to meet. It's the starting point for developing a fund-raising strategy (see page 40).

Over the next year you should review the budget regularly. See what money is coming in. Make sure the people responsible for fund raising give regular report-backs on the progress they're making. That way they can ask for any help they need and you can all be satisfied that everything possible is being done to generate the income you need.

And while you are drawing up the budget for the coming year, why not prepare one for the next three years, or even five years. It gives you a chance to discuss where your organisation is going. Do you want to continue to do the same things in the same way? Will success and prosperity change you? If so, will you be prepared? Will the same people be involved or will it be a totally different set of people with different perspectives on what needs to be done? You need to have one eye to the future if you are to raise money in the longer term. A three or five-year budget need not be very accurate and it does not matter if you don't stick to it. In fact it is not even about financial needs really, so much as an opportunity to develop a long-term perspective on your work.

BUDGETING FOR PROJECTS

You may have got together as a group because you shared a common interest in some aspect of women's lives. You probably made personal donations to cover the initial costs of holding meetings or organising activities on a small scale. But it's likely that sooner or later you will come up with an idea for a special project – such as producing a careers pamphlet for schoolgirls. It may be the project that brought you together in the first place.

The point is that projects generate their own financial requirements above and beyond the costs of holding meetings, sending out the minutes and so on. Projects therefore need separate budgets in addition to the main budget for the organisation or group.

The process of estimating costs is exactly the same as that described above, but in practice it's more complicated. For example, the project may need to be housed, serviced and managed.

It may use space and the rent and rates have to be paid for. There'll be telephone, postage, stationery and printing costs. Accounts will have to be kept. If you employ staff, they may be devoting some of their time to the project both before and after it has got under way.

These 'central' overhead costs must be met from some source, and unless the whole of this cost is already being paid for, each aspect of the organisation's work must contribute something towards the overheads. This 'apportionment' of the overheads of the organisation is necessary if the money to pay for this expenditure is to be found. They are as much a part of the expenditure needed to run the project as any of the costs that will be directly incurred, such as, in our careers pamphlet example, research expenses, printing or publicity material.

You may not be able to persuade donors to pay for apportioned costs, let alone the direct costs, but don't underestimate the importance of accounting for them, and if needs be, use the proceeds from odd fund-raising activities like a sponsored walk or jumble sale to meet them.

WHO DOES WHAT?

Probably the biggest problem is that nobody wants to do the fund raising. Or maybe everyone agrees to take part of the responsibility but they've all got other things to do too and the fund-raising job is always the last on the list.

The consequences are obvious. Everyone feels guilty. Deadlines are missed. You fail to seize opportunities as they arise. Or you run out of money altogether. You create the climate for bad feeling and recrimination which voluntary organisations can ill afford.

Women may have serious doubts about their ability to get results when it comes to raising money, particularly in the face of reactions ranging from, at best, indifference, to, at worst, hostility.

There are ways to cope constructively with these problems. For example, make an effort to find out about the success stories. There are some! The women involved might be able to give you some tips on how to succeed.

If you're trying to raise a large sum of money, people may worry that their life for years will be dominated by this awesome task.

Try to relieve some of these fears by rotating the work. Break down the tasks. Somebody can write the latest batch of letters; someone else can co-ordinate preparation of a leaflet and liaise with the printer; one or two of the other women can attend a meeting with the officers at the Town Hall. Working together dilutes the sense of anxiety that will plague everybody until you score your first success.

It's unlikely you will consider using a professional fund-raiser. If you are a sizeable and long-established organisation you may have the people and resources to allocate this job to a particular member of staff. It's an important job so take extra care in finding the right person to do it.

If you are the finance officer, or if you are a small group of women responsible for fund raising, you may feel at times that at meetings there are always more urgent things on the agenda than your worries. When it comes to discussing fund raising everyone may be feeling tired and there's less concentration. Some of the women might have to leave early. There may come a time when you have to demand that fund raising be taken first, or at least early on in the meeting. Your group must be made to understand the crucial importance of fund raising and that if you are to survive there will be times in the life of any voluntary group when fund raising must take precedence over all other issues. Not everyone in your group will read this book, but get them all to read this paragraph if you're having trouble getting fund raising discussed as a priority.

When you've tackled some of these fundamental problems, try to build your fund-raising effort round the women who will do it, make use of their likes and avoid their dislikes. Nurture the talent that's never had the chance to bloom until now. Make sure that people are provided with sufficient back-up to do the job properly: resources, support, encouragement, and, most importantly, access to decision making.

Start with what's already on offer – the good will and energy of your members, your trustees, your management committee, your supporters. What can they do for you? What skills and contacts do they have? Who do they know who might give you money or materials to get the project off the ground? With any luck you'll end up going off in all sorts of unexpected directions with better results than you might have anticipated.

BUILD YOUR CONTACTS

It is often said that fund raising is 90 per cent who you know and only 10 per cent what you know. The impression is that people who are well connected, who are members of the old boys' network, or maybe wives of the members of the old boys' network, have easy access to the wealthy individuals who are prepared to be tapped for their 'pet charities'. The advantages of such connections are clear. One Oxford men's college, for example, with a fund-raising target of £2 million, raised £750,000 from three individuals before making a wider public appeal.

The relative wealth of men and the ease with which they can pull strings and cream off spare cash from all sorts of places for the projects and causes they deem worthy may make many women boiling mad. But if contacts are 90 per cent of what it's all about, it may be a case of 'if you can't beat them, join them'.

Build your professional and political contacts: the local councillors and town hall officers who process and decide on grants, the trust administrators you deal with, the company directors you can persuade to help you, the local people who will organise fund-raising events for you. For most groups these are the contacts most worth cultivating.

When you start out you might not know anyone, and no one knows if you are capable of doing a good job. So try to meet the people you are seeking funds from. Invite them to come and see what you are doing. Go to conferences, open meetings, workshops and seminars where you might meet them and introduce yourself. Work out who you need to influence and find someone who is well placed to do the influencing. Then ask them. Make sure they know enough about what you are doing and support it themselves, and make sure they understand exactly what it is they are expected to do and who they are to liaise with.

CHARITABLE STATUS

It is worth considering applying to become a registered charity. The main advantages are certain tax privileges; eligibility for financial help from other charities; and a good public image which helps when fund raising. Charitable status enables individuals to covenant, i.e. pledge to donate a particular amount each year for over three years, and you can reclaim the tax that has already been deducted on the donation. Disadvantages of charitable status are that a group's objects must all be charitable; there are restrictions on changing the objects and on dissolving the group; and the Charity Commissioners in England and Wales (and the Inland Revenue in Scotland and Northern Ireland) have controlling powers.

In order to be registered as a charity, an organisation must be formally established for exclusively charitable purposes by means of a suitable governing document such as a trust deed, constitution, set of rules, etc. This document should declare the objects for which the organisation was founded and make provision for its administration. The Charity Commissioners like to see the draft of the governing document before issuing an application form for registration. Try to recruit a friendly local solicitor or law centre worker to help you draw up a document. Don't hold back on applying for funding until registration is confirmed. On average, it takes from three to six months, although it can take longer. Most donors who restrict their giving to registered charities will usually consider you while your application for charitable status is being processed.

Any group seeking charitable status has to satisfy the Charity Commissioners that it fits into one or more of the four categories of charitable activity: relief of poverty, advancement of education (not confined to academic teaching), the advancement of religion and some other purposes beneficial to the community. There are restrictions on political activities by charities and also on commercial activity (although there are various ways round this such as setting up a trading company which covenants its profits back to the charity). Highly committed pressure groups which are unable to register may be able to set up a charitable sister organisation to act as a financial siphon (e.g. the National Council for Civil Liberties and the Cobden Trust).

Advice on obtaining charitable status is available from NCVO's Legal Department (see page 117 for address).

DEVELOPING A STRATEGY AND SPENDING MONEY TO MAKE MONEY

Map out a possible strategy for fund raising and work out how much expense it will entail. If you are totally penniless will you be able to meet those initial expenses through collections amongst yourselves? Can the members of your group afford to carry the cost of telephone calls, stationery, postage and photocopying? If you are going to start with a fund-raising event such as a jumble sale, are you sure you'll make enough to cover the cost of hiring a hall, producing posters, and making a few telephone calls? It is inevitable that in trying to raise money you are going to spend some, so be sure that your strategy is sound and that you are not going to end up out of pocket.

Your income in cash and kind is likely to come from a combination of the following: statutory sources, including local and central government and quangos, charitable trusts, companies, membership subscriptions, support groups, other voluntary organisations, donations in kind, individual cash donations, and fund-raising events. For more details on these sources see chapters 4, 5 and 6.

Statutory funding

You may feel you have a strong chance of getting some public money either from your local council or some other government body. Try to secure that first. Charitable trusts tend to expect it. Find out which council committees make grants and whether you fit into any of their categories. You should be able to get this information through the committee clerks. Before applying to other government bodies, get hold of the application forms and guidelines, and ask for advice from officials.

Trusts

Make a list of the charitable trusts which might support you. Find out about their policies, their track record for making grants, how much, how often, who to? What are their deadlines? Do they impose any conditions? Tailor your application to the specific trust in question and supply a set of accounts if possible.

Companies

When you buy anything, such as stationery, furniture or office equipment, always ask for a discount. Try to get donations in kind. Use businesses owned by women for your purchases. For cash donations, apply to firms with a strong presence or interest in your area. Pay particular attention to firms which either manufacture products bought by women or which rely on women's labour.

Membership subscriptions

If you are a membership organisation, estimate the value of the subscriptions from the total figure and the costs incurred in administering the membership, such as production and mailing of a newsletter or minutes.

Support groups and other voluntary organisations

Consider setting up a support group of people who will make some sort of effort to fund-raise when called upon. Can you expect any other voluntary organisations to adopt you? Some women's aid refuges have received a lot of support in this way.

Donations in kind

It's not just companies which are in a position to make donations in kind. Professionals such as solicitors, accountants, journalists, graphic designers, photographers, etc. may all be prepared to offer their skills.

Cash donations

Appealing for cash donations can bring results, but it depends on publicity and contacts. Again, you need to consider the costs involved in producing an appeal leaflet, for instance, administering the donations and sending out receipts, or organising a launch event.

Fund-raising events

Raising at least some of your money from your own supporters or the people likely to benefit from your existence can be very worthwhile. The amounts raised may be small, but the effort put into this kind of fund raising pays off in many different ways. Not least it impresses other potential donors to be able to say 'We're not just doing this for ourselves. The people out there want us to survive.'

Whatever combination you choose, the main thing is to try to match yourselves with the most probable sources of support. Don't send a standard letter to every single body you can think of. It might involve more work, but it is worth singling out a manageable number of potential donors, researching their policies and procedures, and nurturing contact with them over a period of time.

This is the time when you should also consider whom you will not accept money from. You may have qualms about asking, say, a cosmetics firm for a donation. On the other hand, you may think that a company so dependent on women's money should return some of it to women's own projects. A few years ago, the staff of a women's magazine had a long discussion about whether or not to accept a grant from the Equal Opportunities Commission, after they had applied and been successful. Work out your rules in advance, but be sure you are not being unnecessarily cautious.

And think about the future. Use fund-raising methods which you can repeat. Try to secure grants which are renewable. Make an annual appeal to your members. Organise a sponsored walk each year. Whatever will stand you in good stead over the years is to be preferred to a one-off activity. You'll do it better each time round.

Strike a good balance between different types of funding. Over-dependence on one large grant can plunge you into a financial crisis when circumstances change.

HINTS ON HOW TO ASK FOR MONEY

You don't get what you don't ask for. So ask. Be persistent and be resilient. If people turn you down, they are not rejecting you personally. You may have applied at the wrong time or for more than they could afford to give. Find out why you were rejected and if there is anything you can do to increase your chances of success next time. Go back to them a second time unless you know for sure that they definitely can't or won't support you. People admire persistence and it really does pay.

Ask for enough. A common problem is not to take all your costs into account when working out how much you need. If a trust has a policy of making grants around the £2,000 mark but you only need £1,500, work out an application that does come to £2,000. Otherwise you might be doing yourself out of £500. Set your membership subscriptions at a realistic level.

Don't limit where you look for money. You may try the obvious sources but still find you're short. People can raise money from almost anything. One women's charity regularly makes £100 by raffling a cake. Be imaginative. People respond to zany ideas.

Most donors prefer to give money to something specific so that they know what their money is being spent on. When you approach trusts, in particular, think of something specific you want the money for: a piece of equipment, production of a video, sponsorship of a delegation to an international women's conference.

Match your needs to the policies and interests of potential donors by devising projects which highlight aspects of your work. If you are running summer holiday playschemes for children from one-parent families, apply to a trust interested in the theatre for the costs of a stock of dressing-up clothes and props. Some potential donors may not be the most obvious, but look hard at your work to see if there's anything about it which might interest them.

Give potential donors a choice over how big a donation to make. Give them a mental picture of what each level of donation would buy. Don't say 'will' buy. You might find your hands tied too tightly. But if you find you are successful with two applications to pay for the same thing, explain to one of the donors what's happened and ask if you might spend the money on something else. In 99 per cent of cases they will be happy to agree.

MAINTAINING MORALE AND GOOD PUBLIC RELATIONS

Fund raising is not just about raising money. It is a two-stage process. You have to convince people about the importance of your work. Then you have to ask them to support it.

To convince people of the importance of what you are doing you yourself have to understand its importance. You have to believe in it, then you have to 'sell' it to other people. What are you 'selling'?

What are its key 'selling points'?

Think about why the problem or need you are concerned with is important and why your organisation is worth backing. Don't beg. Rehearse the arguments. If most people felt the way you do about what you are doing there possibly wouldn't be any need for you to do what you are doing.

Most donors in a position to hand out money to women like yourselves receive hundreds of applications. You have to show why they should back you and your own enthusiasm is the key thing. If you are worried about competing with other women's groups for cash, talk to them about it and see if you can solve your problems through co-operation rather than competition. It can also be hard for women to ask for money in the face of competing appeals from other causes such as Ethiopian famine relief or the Campaign for Nuclear Disarmament, but it's necessary. Problems which make our other preoccupations seem minor will always attract money, so keep trying for your group's own modest slice of the cake.

Keep up the morale of your members by holding regular report-backs. Organise an annual get-together, a social occasion for your own pleasure, and reflect on the successes you've achieved. Be philosophical and take a long-term view of what you're doing. There's no doubt about it, fund raising is hard work and the odds often seem stacked against women's voluntary organisations in particular. But don't let your enthusiasm flag. Don't forget, you have the motivation to put in time and effort for someone else's benefit. That impresses people and it will pay off. Some of you will get disheartened from time to time. It's bound to happen. But don't let that mood dominate. There'll be other people in the group who will feel just as enthusiastic as ever. Let their optimism carry you through.

Maintaining good public relations is an investment which will also carry you through the gloomy patches. Try to get some favourable coverage in your local paper or on your local radio and television stations. Organise a regular stall in your local shopping precinct. Hold open meetings for potential supporters. Keep people informed about your progress. It will all make you feel needed, renewing your determination to get results.

4 The Major Statutory Sources of Funding

There are many legal powers under which government can distribute funds to the voluntary sector. What is as important as the power is the policy – how much money there is to give to whom and for what. This chapter provides some basic information on these statutory sources of funding, their powers and policies.

LOCAL GOVERNMENT

Local government can be an extremely important source of funds for local organisations and, indeed, many organisations or groups feel they should be supported in this way, particularly if they are offering a service or meeting a need.

There is not just one local authority in your area. Everywhere, except in the main metropolitan regions where the county councils have been abolished, there is both a district council and a county council. In London the district council is known as the borough council. In some areas there is a smaller unit, the parish or town council. In Scotland the county council equivalent is the regional council and in Northern Ireland the whole structure of government is different, with most functions being carried out by a central government department, the Northern Ireland Office.

45

How to Go About It

There is also the district health authority which is responsible for local health service provision and there are other local bodies which can give grants: the local education authority (which in most areas will be the county council; it is the borough council in outer London and the Inner London Education Authority in inner London), and the police authority which may be able to give small grants for community and crime prevention schemes.

You need to know which authority is responsible for what aspect of local life and how it organises its committees. It is the committees to which applications are made. Your chances of getting a grant will depend on their attitude towards voluntary organisations and the amount of money they have available, which will vary considerably.

A number of local councils now have women's committees or their equivalent. In 1985, these were the London boroughs of Hackney, Greenwich, Lewisham, Southwark, Camden, Brent, Islington and Haringey, and Aberdeen, Basildon, Birmingham, Edinburgh, Leeds, Manchester, Newcastle upon Tyne, Stirling and Wolverhampton. You should make direct enquiries to your local council on whether or not these committees exist, with any grant-making budgets, in your area.

The legal basis for local authority support

A local authority must spend its money for the benefit of the people in its area. The 1972 Local Government Act sets out the main permitted powers of a local authority. Sections 111 and 137 give broad general powers which permit it to do virtually anything which is of local benefit. But s. 137 funds are limited to 2p in the rate and not all local authorities even use these funds in this way. Up to 1981/82 just over half (53 per cent) of local authorities in England and Wales had used s. 137 and only 21 authorities in the whole of the UK spent more than 50 per cent of the amount possible. Only four spent over 80 per cent.

There is a variety of other legislation under which grants can be made. It is worth being able to quote the legislation exactly. Often the local authorities themselves don't realise they have other powers enabling them to fund the voluntary sector which can offer greater flexibility than s. 137.

Relevant legislation

Child Care Act 1980 (s. 1): Grants for activities which diminish the need for children to be taken into care, kept in care or brought before a juvenile court.

Education Act 1944 (s. 53): Grants for a wide range of activities benefiting people receiving education.

Health Services and Public Health Act 1968 (ss. 44, 45, 65):
Grants for accommodation for persons in need of care or attention, for the welfare of old people, for voluntarily-run health and social services schemes where the authority itself must or may provide a service.

Housing Act 1985 (s. 73):
Grants, premises, goods and services of staff for organisations concerned with homelessness.

Local Government Act 1972 (s. 142): Grants for activities which publicise local services and local government matters affecting the area; (s. 145): Grants for entertainment and the arts; (s. 201): Support for organisations providing consumer advice.

Local Government (Miscellaneous Provisions) Act 1976 (s. 19): Grants, loans or premises for recreational purposes; (s. 38): Spare computer capacity or facilities.

London Government Act 1948 (s. 47): Grants towards the welfare of children.

National Assistance Act 1948 (ss. 29 and 30):
Support for groups helping the handicapped.

National Health Service Act 1977 (s. 21):
Accommodation for voluntary organisations' employees working on the care of mothers and young children, the prevention and after-care of illness and other services; (s. 23): Facilities for groups providing services which a district health authority can also provide.

None of the legislation distinguishes between a 'charity' and a 'voluntary body'. In theory local authorities can give support to either. In practice many prefer that recipients of grants are registered charities.

Many of the grants to voluntary organisations are made under the general powers contained in s. 137 of the 1972 Local Government Act. But knowing the specific powers can be quite helpful in deciding what to ask for and how to discuss your application with officers.

Different types of local authority support

A local authority can provide support in a number of ways:

The voluntary organisation as agent of the council. A grant may be given for a voluntarily-run service which the local authority is legally obliged to provide, such as meals-on-wheels, day centres for elderly people and facilities for under-fives. Grants can also be made to groups providing information and advice which help the local authority to carry out its functions more effectively; and to groups carrying out developmental work on behalf of the authority or work that complements and supplements its own.

Support to 'agency' bodies usually involves a long-term relationship with the local authority.

The local authority as customer. In certain situations – usually to do with special housing needs – the local authority can buy a service from a voluntary organisation in order to meet its own legal obligations.

Grant aid. Voluntary organisations may be receiving grant aid either for capital projects or for specific one-off revenue costs (such as for equipment or a short-term project) or towards running costs. The grant will be made because the work of the voluntary organisation is of local benefit. In most cases local authority grant aid will only be a contribution to funding. The remainder will have to be found elsewhere.

Rate relief. Under the General Rates Act 1967, a charity is entitled to 50 per cent relief on its premises. This is mandatory relief. The local authority is obliged to give it. A further discretionary rate relief can be given on the remaining 50 per cent.

Bulk purchase of supplies. Under the Local Authority Goods and Services Act 1980, a local authority has the power to make available to certain public bodies, including some voluntary organisations, bulk purchased goods, technical assistance, use of vehicles and maintenance work on premises.

Small grants. Small grants may be awarded through a Community Chest fund, a mayor's appeal fund, a town lottery fund or grant-making trusts administered by the local authority.

Section 11 funding. This is a central government subsidy for certain types of projects which meet the special needs of ethnic minority communities, and in very limited circumstances it can be used to support projects run by voluntary organisations. Black women might be interested in finding out more about it but should not see it as the answer to funding problems. The money covers salary costs of local authority staff employed on special projects benefiting Commonwealth immigrants whose language or customs differ from those of the rest of the community. The local education department or social services department will have details, or you can get the current guidelines from Room T1282, I Division, Home Office, 50 Queen Anne's Gate, London SW1 9AT.

Joint action. Many local authorities are now teaming up with voluntary organisations to work on local economic development. This type of 'partnership' is particularly attractive when tackling areas neglected by more traditional economic development methods. Women could therefore benefit from joint action, which also has the advantage of being a good way of attracting matching funds from the European Social Fund (see page 65) where a close relationship with government is vital to successful applications. Ask your local council or CVS about it.

Underspend. Local authorities have pre-arranged timetables and procedures for making grants. But there are times when they need to give money away in a hurry in order to spend their full budget allocation before the end of the financial year, 31 March. February is often a good month to apply in order to take advantage of this.

Post-abolition funding

Abolition of the metropolitan county councils and the Greater London Council on 1 April 1986 has removed a complete tier of local government which was a significant source of funding for the voluntary sector. However, some funds will continue to be made available via successor bodies, but even so the picture remains gloomy.

The main provision for the seven areas affected (see chapter 2, page 22) is that the Department of the Environment will make £40 million available over the next four years to the borough and district councils for groups previously funded by the counties. Over the four years the contribution from the DoE will taper off as the proportion the borough/district councils fund increases. By the financial year 1990/1991, there will be no more central government help towards transitional funding and the borough/district councils will be under no obligation to wholly support projects which have previously benefited. Applications under this scheme, known as transitional funding, have closed and no further applications will be invited between now and 1990/91.

The Local Government Act 1985, which abolished the GLC and MCCs, also allowed for county-wide grants schemes with the aim of helping organisations covering more than one borough or district council area. These collective schemes are not mandatory, that is to say the councils are under no obligation to set them up. They can be set up by a simple majority of the councils in each metropolitan county area, but thereafter grants have to be approved by a two-thirds majority.

In London the county-wide scheme is being administered by a unit housed by Richmond Borough Council and it has become known as the 'Richmond Scheme'. To be eligible for funding under this scheme, an organisation must either serve the whole of

49

How to Go About It

London, or provide an innovative service which could potentially benefit the whole of London, or be involved in work which forms part of a Londonwide strategy approved jointly by the boroughs. You will not be eligible if your group provides only local services even if the services are provided in several boroughs; if you are engaged in party political activities; if you are a national organisation not specifically aimed at Londoners; or if you are a group whose prime aim is to persuade central government to change national policy.

The Grant Unit at Twickenham is divided into four categories:

- housing
- social services
- employment, social education, environment, transport, culture and recreation
- co-ordinating bodies, advice and information, community projects

At the time of writing (January 1986) full details were not available. It seems likely, however, that two major meetings of the governing body will be held each year, one in July to determine strategies and priorities and one in November to take budget decisions.

Full details of how the scheme operates are available from the London Boroughs Grant Unit, PO Box 57, Twickenham, Mx TW1 TW1 3AZ,

tel. 01-891 0381/892 4616/ 892 4290.

For details of the collective schemes in the other metropolitan county areas, where they have been set up, you should contact the Co-ordinating Committee which is made up of representatives of the district councils. Telephone your local district council and ask for Information or Public Relations who should be able to put you in touch with the officers servicing the Co-ordinating Committee. It is possible that not all co-ordinating committees will have set up collective grants schemes, but there is definitely one in the Greater Manchester area and the lead authority is Manchester City Council.

There is also to be a new trust fund 'to provide assistance to voluntary bodies whose activities benefit Londoners'. The initial endowment for this new charitable trust is to be at least £10 million, which will come from the sale of GLC assets. The Government also expects contributions to be made from private and commercial sources. Revenue to be dispersed in grants may be around £600,000, but it is unlikely to be available before 1987/88. As yet there are no details available about policies or procedures but the trust is to be administered by the City Parochial Foundation, 10 Fleet Street, London EC4Y 1AU, tel. 01-353 5678/9.

50

How to succeed in getting a grant

Probably the most important factor affecting your chances of getting a grant is the amount of money available. This varies enormously. The GLC in its last year was giving £40–50 million in grants to voluntary organisations while some local authorities give very little at all. Policies also vary from area to area on the kind of grant given.

Find out who is getting what, how much and what for. The information should be publicly available in the minutes of the committee meetings.

Plan ahead. There will normally be a timetable for considering grant applications so you will do better to choose the best time to apply to fit in with council procedures. For a grant for the year starting 1 April next you will probably need to draw up an outline with a draft budget to be discussed with council officers. The formal application would go in during September or October in order to make its way through the committee structure for a decision by February or March.

Decisions may be taken on factors such as the following:

Charitable status. Some councils will only give to registered charities, or at least to bodies which can supply audited accounts.

Credibility. The better able you are to demonstrate that you are an effective, well-run organisation, the easier it will be to get support.

Community benefit. Round up as many facts and figures as you can on how the local community benefits from your proposal, such as numbers of people, who they are, why they need you.

Community support. If a local authority has to choose between two equally useful organisations, the one which is more firmly rooted in the community is the one they will choose to support. Supply evidence of membership, volunteers, cash donations, etc.

Value for money. When money is short, the local authority will want to provide the most comprehensive service at least cost. How can you demonstrate the value for money your work represents?

Relationship to other services. Local authorities want to support services which complement or supplement those which they provide directly. So it is important to have a clear understanding of how your project fits in with existing provision and why it is important that the gap should be filled.

Evidence of need. Avoid the rhetoric of phrases like 'desperate need', or 'serious problem'. Try to quantify the need in facts and figures. Do your own survey. Use information from the local authorities' own surveys, reports, committee

51

papers. Use policy statements made by the council and councillors themselves.

Other sources of funding. If you can or are planning to attract funds from other sources, this will be a great help.

If you do get a grant towards your running costs, you will need to think about whether the local authority will continue to support you. You have to keep convincing them of the value of your work with a fresh application each year.

If you have the time and money to spare, try to do some of the following: circulate your annual report and accounts to local councillors. Involve them in your activities. Invite the mayor to open your jumble sale, or start your annual sponsored walk. Keep people informed about what you are doing – the staff who liaise with voluntary organisations, the director of the department, committee chair and members responsible for your area of work, your ward councillors, the party leaders. Keep in touch with local bodies such as the council for voluntary service which are seen as legitimate representatives of the voluntary sector.

CENTRAL GOVERNMENT

Central government funding on the whole is not given to local projects. It is chiefly there to help national organisations with administration costs. But central government will support local activities if they are innovatory with potential for development on a national scale, or if action is required by central government to help get things moving locally or to deal with a particular social problem.

If you are a national organisation, you should be thinking about asking for support. But what is a 'national organisation'? It's not always clear. Certainly you don't have to be London-based. Nor do you need to be called the 'National Association of . . .' The real test is whether you feel you are giving a national lead, whether you are countrywide in character, and if you accept enquiries from anywhere in the country.

It is also unclear what innovatory projects are. If you feel that the work you are doing is important, that the problem is widespread and newly identified, or if you're using new methods to deal with it which are capable of being repeated elsewhere, then you might stand a chance of persuading central government to back you.

Central government will also back activities tackling particular problems in an area. The aim is to provide temporary funding (normally up to three years) to get projects going which then gives

them time to find other sources of support.
The main government departments you should consider approaching are listed below.

Department of the Environment
2 Marsham Street
London SW1P 3EB
The DoE gives grants for local voluntary action to improve the environment, for experimental projects, and for groups concerned with improving the appearance of or renewed use of derelict buildings or land. It also administers the Urban Programme which is discussed separately (see page 63).

Department of Health and Social Security
Alexander Fleming House
Elephant and Castle
London SE1 6BY
The DHSS is a major source of grant aid to the kinds of projects run by women. More than 350 voluntary organisations received a total of £30 million in grants in 1984/85, and the majority were paid under s. 64 of the Health Services and Public Health Act 1968. This is a general scheme designed to help support the central costs of national voluntary organisations. Grants have been made to groups including the Association of Carers (£23,000), Centre for Ethnic Minorities Health Studies (£20,000), Maternity Alliance (£30,000) Rape Counselling and Research Project (£23,953), Sexual and Personal Relationships of the Disabled (£32,000) and Widows Advisory Trust (£12,000). Other schemes are designed to encourage new and better ways of working in a particular field.

Funds are also available through:

Intermediate Treatment Initiative, which is designed to prevent young people from being taken into care or custody. Details available from Intermediate Treatment Fund, 33 King Street, London WC2E 8JD, tel: 01-379 6171.

Drugs Misuse Initiative, which is designed to improve services to drug misusers. Details available from Branch CS2(B), DHSS at above address.

Opportunities For Volunteering, which is a scheme to help projects providing opportunities for unemployed people to do voluntary work in the health or personal social services. Details available from Consortium for Opportunities for Volunteering, c/o NCVO, 26 Bedford Square, London WC1B 3HU, tel: 01-636 4066.

Under-Fives Initiative, which supports schemes helping families with pre-school children, especially lone-parent families and low-income families and innovative self-help schemes originating in the Black and Asian communities. Details available from National Council of Voluntary Child Care Organisations, 8 Wakley Street, London EC1V 7QE, tel: 01-278 9441.

Joint Finance and *Care in the Community* which fund projects helping to bring people out of hospital into the community. Details available from the district health authority and/or local social services department.

Home Office
50 Queen Anne's Gate
London SW1H 9AT
Grants for marriage guidance work, for residential or day-care projects for the rehabilitation and care of ex-offenders. It also houses the Voluntary Services Unit (see page 117).

Other government departments giving grants are:

Department of Education and Science
Elizabeth House
York Road
London SE1 7PH
The DES is responsible for schools, universities, adult education, the youth service, the arts, museums and libraries.

Department of Trade and Industry
1 Victoria Street
London SW1H 0ET
Responsible for trade and industry generally, for the promotion of new industry, for consumer affairs and information technology.

Department of Employment
Caxton House
Tothill Street
London SW1H 9NF
The DE oversees the Manpower Services Commission and is the siphon for applications to the European Community Social Fund. Both of these are discussed separately.

Scottish Office
New St Andrews House
Edinburgh EH1 3SZ

Welsh Office
Cathays Park
Cardiff CF1 3NQ

Northern Ireland Office
Stormont Castle
Belfast BT4 3ST

Each of the main departments will have a liaison officer dealing with voluntary organisations. You can either contact the department direct or first contact the Home Office Voluntary Services Unit (VSU) which will guide you to the appropriate department with the name, address and telephone number of the person to contact. The VSU can also fund organisations where responsibility for the area of work does not fit in with any one government department or where that department does not at the present time have the powers to make funding available.

Government spending, like local authority spending, is on an annual cycle. But normally there will not be any formal procedure for handling grant applications. You must make your case and apply. If you are turned down, reasons may be given, and it may be that next year or at some future time you could apply again. This time try to find ways round the previous objections.

QUANGOS

Central government money is also distributed by non-governmental organisations – quangos.

Equal Opportunities Commission
Overseas House
Quay Street
Manchester M3 3HN
Tel. 061-833 9244

The EOC is the quango whose responsibilities are most relevant to women's needs. It is not, however, a body solely devoted to women. Rather it is there to promote equality between the sexes, and the interpretation of that responsibility depends to a great extent on the Commissioners who are government-appointed. Groups running rape crisis services for women, for instance, will understand the frustration arising from a too narrow definition of the EOC's role. It is not sufficient for projects to benefit women for them to attract grant aid from the EOC. They must also help eliminate sex discrimination or promote equality of opportunity.

For that reason and for several others which we will explain, you should not expect too much from the EOC, even though it seems like the most obvious place for a woman's organisation to start when looking for public funds. All the same, the EOC probably values women's voluntary activity more than any other official body.

If your work is likely to have lasting significance, then you should try to form a relationship with the EOC even if you are unsuccessful with a grant application. There are other ways in which the EOC can support you and enhance your work and, of course, you should be trying to influence the Commission so that through them, central government gets to hear about women's needs and demands.

The EOC is empowered to make grants under s. 54 of the Sex Discrimination Act 1975, which stipulates research and educational activities which work for the elimination of discrimination, promote equal opportunity between men and women and keep under review the Sex Discrimination and Equal Pay Acts.

The EOC also has a budget to fund conferences organised by

voluntary organisations. Applications for conference grants are considered throughout the year but must be received at least eight weeks before the event. Grants rarely exceed £500.

The EOC's annual grant-making budget was £71,000 in 1985/86, a minute amount when set alongside the funds available to other grant-making bodies, let alone the financial needs of women's groups, voluntary organisations and individuals seeking support.

Applications are processed by the Voluntary Organisations Unit. If you are considering applying to the EOC, you should ring up and have a chat with the staff in the VO Unit who will give you an idea of your eligibility and your chances. They will also give you guidance on filling in the application form.

In 1985/86 (up to November) there were four grant-making rounds, but this could change in subsequent years. The types of projects funded tend to incorporate new ideas or to look at problems in new ways. They may be supported because they tie in with the EOC's agreed priorities or because they will achieve useful results in an area in which the EOC itself does not have the resources to become involved. Locally-based projects will be considered if it can be demonstrated that the outcome would also have some impact nationally.

One potential problem for many groups is that projects must not breach the Sex Discrimination Act, so if you intend to use EOC finance to recruit only women workers or to run a women-only conference, you may not be successful. However, there is a section of the Act which allows a non-profit-making voluntary body to restrict to one sex both its membership and the benefits, facilities and services it provides to its members. It is also lawful for a voluntary body to confer its benefits on one sex generally, provided this is the main object of the organisation.

Any group applying for assistance towards the cost of an activity restricted to one sex must supply the EOC with evidence of its status as a voluntary body, such as a written constitution or an introductory leaflet stating the group's aims and organisation. Ask the VO Unit for guidance.

Grants are normally made for one year only and can be as small as £200. The average grant is about £5,000, covering the cost of a part-time worker and other expenses. An application will rarely be successful if a full-time salary for more than one worker is requested. You will deal with officers of the EOC but ultimately, the decision on who gets grants is made by the Commissioners themselves and all grants are closely monitored.

Examples of grants made in

recent years are:

- £4,000 to Stramullion Co-operative, Edinburgh, to help cover the cost of updating *Scottish Woman's Place*, a guide to women's rights in Scotland.
- £5,745 to a Sussex University academic to investigate the effect of company sponsorship on women studying engineering.
- £7,112 towards the launch of a new magazine for Asian women, *MUKTI*, produced by the Asian Women's Resource Centre, London.

The EOC has published a full list of the grants it has made since it was established. It might be an idea to ask for a copy to assess your own chances of success.

The EOC has also been working on identifying alternative and additional sources of funding for projects in the equality field. Contact the VO Unit for advice on where else you might be able to look for support.

Commission for Racial Equality
Elliott House
10–12 Allington Street
London SW1E 5EH
Tel. 01-828 7022

The CRE is the quango concerned with ethnic minorities. Again, their grant-making funds are very limited and black women's groups should not automatically turn to the CRE despite it being an obvious starting point. One consolation though is that some of the more liberal charitable trusts and some government funds such as the Urban Programme recognise the needs of the black communities for finance and have developed explicit policies to spend money in this way.

Total funds available from the CRE for grants to voluntary organisations were just over £1 million in 1983/84. Of this, £400,000 was already earmarked for projects being funded over several years.

It is a condition of the CRE that the applicant must be able to show that no alternative sources of funds are available. So you will have to try elsewhere and fail before you have any chance of success with the CRE. At least the CRE is prepared to help you apply elsewhere so it is worth contacting them anyway. Write to the Field Services Department.

The CRE gives Project Aid for projects requiring initial funding to establish themselves, and self-help grants for groups working on counselling/advice giving, literacy and other educational work, and vocational training targetted at alienated black young people between the ages of 13 and 25. The kinds of activities which attract funding are youth training and counselling; employment projects including projects designed to improve the employment opportunities for vulnerable groups within minority communities; legal and advice centres; race relations training such as short courses and seminars of immigration legislation, or combatting institutional racism; projects working with elderly members of ethnic minorities; ethnic arts including carnivals; conferences; and publications.

The CRE is adopting a regional focus to its funding. Each region has its own priorities for what it will support locally, and you should discuss your proposal with the Regional Fieldwork Office before submitting your application. The CRE also funds national activities direct from its Head Office. Applications are considered once a year and should be submitted by the end of October, at the latest.

In addition to the EOC and CRE, there are a number of other quangos which are sources of finance and worth considering, depending on the type of work you are doing.

Arts Council
105 Piccadilly
London W1V 0AV
Tel. 01-629 9495

Scottish Arts Council
19 Charlotte Square
Edinburgh EH2 4DF

Welsh Arts Council
Museum Place
Cardiff CF1 3NX

Regional Arts Associations

Eastern Arts
8–9 Bridge Street
Cambridge CB2 1UA

East Midlands Arts
Mountfields House
Forest Road
Loughborough LE11 3HU

Greater London Arts
25–31 Tavistock Place
London WC1H 9SF

Lincolnshire and Humberside Arts
St Hugh's
Newport
Lincoln LN1 3DN

Merseyside Arts
Bluecoat Chambers
School Lane
Liverpool L1 3BX

Northern Arts
10 Osborne Terrace
Newcastle upon Tyne NE2 1NZ

North West Arts
12 Harter Street
Manchester M1 6HY

Southern Arts
19 Southgate Street
Winchester SO23 7EB

South East Arts
9–10 Crescent Road
Tunbridge Wells TN1 2LU

South West Arts
Bradninch Place, Gandy Street
Exeter EX4 3LS

West Midlands Arts
Lloyds Bank Chambers
Market Street
Stafford ST16 2ZP

The Major Statutory Sources of Funding

Yorkshire Arts
Glyde House
Glydegate
Bradford BD5 0BQ

Information and advice for ethnic minority arts projects can be obtained from the Minorities Arts Advisory Service, Beauchamp Lodge, 2 Warwick Crescent, London W2 6NE.

The annual report of the regional arts associations will give you an idea of the kinds of grants they make.

British Council
65 Davies Street
London W1Y 2AA
The British Council funds exchanges between groups of young people and similar groups in Europe and the Commonwealth. For further information contact the Exchange Department. The Visiting Arts Unit can provide funds for visiting arts organisations.

British Film Institute
127 Charing Cross Road
London WC2 0EA
Grants towards the production of films and videos, for educational projects and some cinema projects.

British Library
2 Sheraton Street
London W1V 4BH
Grants for research and development projects in library and information services, normally cataloguing and conservation.

Countryside Commission
John Dower House
Crescent Place
Cheltenham GL5 3RA
Grants for conservation, enhancement of and provision of facilities for the enjoyment of the countryside.

Crafts Council
12 Waterloo Place
London SW1Y 4AU

Development Commission
11 Cowley Street
London SW1P 3NA
Grants to promote community initiatives and economic development in rural areas and towards the capital costs of adapting or extending buildings as village halls.

Nature Conservancy Council
70 Castlegate
Grantham NG31 6SH

Sports Council
16 Upper Woburn Place
London WC1H 0QP

Regional Tourist Boards
c/o English Tourist Board
4 Grosvenor Gardens
London SW1 0DU

Grants and loans towards improvement or provision of tourist amenities.

Housing Corporation
149 Tottenham Court Road
London W1P 0BN
Grants and loans are available to housing associations and voluntary organisations working in particular fields, such as providing short-life accommodation or housing for groups with special needs such as single-parent families, elderly people, ex-offenders and people with disabilities.

This can be an important source of funding for groups involved in housing problems. Advice is available from the National Federation of Housing Associations, 175 Grays Inn Road, London WC1X 8UC, tel. 01-278 6571.

MANPOWER SERVICES COMMISSION

The MSC was established in 1974 to run public employment and training services. It is separate from government but accountable to the Secretary of State for Employment.

The MSC schemes relevant to voluntary organisations are:

- the Community Programme (CP), which aims to help long-term unemployed adults by providing temporary jobs on projects of benefit to the community
- the Voluntary Projects Programme (VPP), which aims to give unemployed people the experience of a variety of voluntary work
- the Youth Training Scheme (YTS), aimed at 16- and 17-year-old school leavers who have failed to find a job.

All the schemes have the restriction that jobs provided must *not* replace work already being done (whether by employees or volunteers), nor put at risk the jobs or training of permanent employees.

MSC money is not grant aid to help you directly. It is money provided to different bodies to help the unemployed. The support is given on the MSC's terms.

The schemes are administered locally so you need to find out as much as possible about the local situation from your area MSC office. The telephone number is in the telephone book.

Community Programme
The Community Programme offers quite large funds for projects of community benefit but there are problems too. The unemployed people taken on to CP schemes can

only work for a year. Long-term funding is not secure, although successful projects are sometimes allowed to continue for another year with new staff. Also, the eligibility conditions were changed in November 1984 so that many married women are no longer eligible for Community Programme places. This rule was challenged in an Industrial Tribunal but the Government appealed and at the time of writing (January 1986) the position of married women on CP schemes is unresolved.

Some groups might find being part of a government-backed employment programme unacceptable, even though the CP's arrangements for part-time work might appear attractive to women.

There are several criteria which projects must meet in order to be successful. These mainly involve ensuring that the projects do not antagonise other interests in the community such as existing businesses, terms and conditions of workers, trade union interests and health and safety standards.

Projects must not involve political activity or have political objectives, including party political action, marches or demonstrations, industrial disputes, or printing or distribution of literature connected with these activities.

There are several different ways of linking with the CP:

- as an independent sponsor who designs a project, gets it approved by the MSC and then runs it
- as a managing agent who takes a block allocation of CP places for people who then work for the agent organisation or are 'sub-contracted' to other organisations
- as an associated sponsor who takes employees from a managing agent rather than directly from the MSC
- as a task patron who is not the employer and does not benefit in any financial way from the arrangement but who can get work done by CP staff who will be paid by a sponsor

The opportunities for benefiting from the CP depend on the local situation. Often there will be a waiting list of projects and it may be quite some time before any new project can get off the ground. At other times it may be possible to start immediately.

A sponsor or agent will be reimbursed in full for all project costs up to certain limits. Wages are covered and operating costs are covered with an annual maximum for each approved place. Managing agents receive an agency fee too. Any further costs have to be found by the sponsoring organisation itself. One problem is that income generated by the organisation's sales, if it has any, will be taken into account when calculating the level of MSC support. You need to discuss this 'claw-back' rule with the MSC and an experienced accountant. There are nearly always ways of getting round it.

If you are interested in the Community Programme, contact the local MSC link officer at an early stage to discuss your plans. Then fill in an application form which you'll also be able to get from your MSC area office. It is referred to the local area manpower board for decision.

Voluntary Projects Programme

The Voluntary Projects Programme exists to provide unemployed people with a constructive activity which might develop their existing skills or provide some form of part-time rehabilitation or work preparation without affecting their entitlement to statutory benefits. It is similar to the Opportunities for Volunteering Scheme funded by the DHSS (see page 53).

It provides a means of putting unemployed people in touch with a variety of community projects, training for volunteers and sources of voluntary work which will benefit the wider community.

For the sponsor, the VPP provides money to pay for the organiser's salary and ancillary expenses, up to a maximum of £75,000. Approved costs include staff costs, premises, materials and equipment, volunteer expenses, promotional costs, insurance charges, postage, stationery, bank fees and vehicle costs.

The minimum period for VPP schemes is six months and the maximum a year. The kinds of schemes which might get approval are centres for unemployed people, adult education classes for unemployed people directed to training for or obtaining work, and recruiting staff to encourage unemployed people to undertake voluntary work.

Find out how and where to apply locally from either your council for voluntary service or the Volunteer Centre, 29 Lower Kings Road, Berkhamsted, Herts HP4 2AB. Regional and national organisations with proposals should apply to MSC Head Office, Employment Service Division, Voluntary Projects Unit, Moorfoot, Sheffield S1 4PQ.

Youth Training Scheme

The Youth Training Scheme is not primarily aimed at voluntary organisations, but some do run Youth Training Schemes.

From April 1986 YTS was extended from one year to two years. This provides a greater emphasis on training and sponsors will be expected to make a greater financial contribution out of their own resources. This means that the YTS will be a more difficult source of funding for all voluntary organisations than it has been in the past.

The scheme will eventually offer a two-year training place for all 16-year-old school leavers, and a similar offer of at least one year for all 17-year-old school leavers.

An organisation wishing to sponsor a YTS scheme must be approved by the MSC Area Board. Some YTS managing agents also manage schemes run by individual organisations. You can get information and advice from your MSC Area Office, the Community Schemes Unit at NCVO (see page 117 for address), or Community Projects Foundation Training Workshop Resource Unit, 60 Highbury Grove, London N5 2AG.

URBAN PROGRAMME

The Urban Programme is a major source of funding for voluntary organisations. It was set up under the Local Government Grants (Social Need) Act 1969 and is administered by the Department of the Environment. It provides a central government subsidy for selected local projects run either by the local authority or by voluntary organisations in areas of special social need. Evidence of social need may be poverty, unemployment, poor housing,

educational disadvantage, poor environment, severe pressure on the social services, and large numbers or a high concentration of disadvantaged people from ethnic minority groups. Projects should aim to alleviate deprivation either directly or indirectly. Priority categories include meeting the needs of ethnic minority groups, economic regeneration and improving the physical environment.

Where Urban Programme funding is available

In general, the areas which stand to attract Urban Programme funding are severely deprived urban centres with a population of 20,000 or more. Certain areas have been designated as priority areas. These are the 'Partnership' and 'Programme' areas.

Partnership Areas
Birmingham • Hackney • Islington • Lambeth • Liverpool • Manchester/Salford • Newcastle/Gateshead

Programme Authorities
Blackburn • Bolton • Bradford • Brent • Coventry • Hammersmith and Fulham • Kingston upon Hull • Knowsley • Leeds • Leicester • Middlesbrough • North Tyneside • Nottingham • Oldham • Rochdale • Sandwell • Sheffield • South Tyneside • Sunderland • Tower Hamlets • Wandsworth • Wirral • Wolverhampton

63

Traditional Urban Programme

The areas eligible for what is known as Traditional Urban Programme funding are:

Barnsley • Bristol • Burnley • Calderdale • Camden • Corby • Derby • Derwentside • Doncaster • Dudley • Ealing • Ellesmere Port • Greenwich • Grimsby • Halton • Haringey • Hartlepool • Hyndburn • Kensington and Chelsea • Kirklees • Langbaurgh • Lewisham • Lincoln • Luton • Newham • Pendle • Plymouth • Preston • Rossendale • Rotherham • St Helens • Scunthorpe • Sedgefield • Sefton • Southwark • Stockton • Stoke • Tameside • Trafford • Walsall • Waltham Forest • Wear Valley • West Lancashire • Westminster • Wigan • The Wrekin

Support is available for industrial, commercial, transport, environmental, social, educational and recreational projects. Projects set up for religious or party political purposes do not qualify. Each year guidelines are given for the year's priorities. Over the past few years more importance has been given to environmental and industrial/commercial schemes. Most voluntary groups will probably be looking for support for social welfare/educational projects so there is a lot of competition. Separate funding is available, however, for holiday projects, in particular for children at risk, handicapped children and their parents, single-parent families and children from ethnic minority groups.

The DoE pays 75 per cent of approved costs with the balance coming from the local authority. Applications should be made to the local authority which chooses a shortlist of about 10 to forward to the DoE. Only about 30 per cent of the projects submitted to the DoE receive support.

In general, small-scale low-cost projects are favoured. Capital costs of projects exceeding £160,000, and revenue costs exceeding £40,000 per annum, will not normally be approved. Where a project generates income there is a claw-back rule, although it is possible to find ways round it. Where a project may be eligible for other types of statutory grant, such as Sports Council grants or British Film Institute funding, support is available from the Urban Programme but you will be excluded from applying to the other bodies.

How to apply

Application procedures for Partnership and Programme grants vary from area to area. For the Traditional Urban Programme you should get hold of the annual Urban Programme circular as soon as it is issued which is usually in August. Your local authority or council for voluntary service should be able to help you and give you advice on whether your project is likely to be eligible. Fill in the form and submit it in good time. The application will be assessed on official indications of deprivation so you should include evidence of this from the census and other central and local government reports and surveys. Lobby your ward councillors and committee members who will be making the initial decision on your application. It may help also to tell your local MP about the application. She/he may be able to influence the DoE which makes the final decision.

Keep an eye out for announcements about future arrangements for the Urban Programme and try to prepare any applications well in advance of closing dates. If at first you don't succeed, try again the following year.

EUROPEAN ECONOMIC COMMUNITY

Often an organisation looking for new sources of money says 'What about the EEC?' It's often hard to find out what's available, let alone whether you qualify. There's a lot of bureaucracy involved but there are organisations which have stuck with it and been able to get quite substantial amounts of money. It pays to think big. This section may help you decide whether it's worth your while to apply to the EEC.

European Social Fund

The European Social Fund is a major source of support for voluntary organisations. It is a funny name because it's not 'social' at all in the sense that we understand the word. Its aim is to 'improve the employment opportunities for workers in the Common Market and to contribute thereby to raising the standard of living'. At present the bulk of the money is spent on training schemes. Some of the priorities have been particularly concerned with women, but the separate category for women's schemes was abolished in 1984. Women's projects, though still a priority, now have to compete with schemes for the under-25s and proposals for training and job creation in the depressed areas. However, several schemes run for women have benefited, for example:

- Nottinghamshire Women's Training Scheme, an experimental project designed to meet the needs of adult women for whom more traditional forms of education have proved unsuccessful. The ESF contribution to the running costs is £352,000 over two and a half years.
- Haringey Women's Training

65

and Education Centre, which aims to bring new opportunities to women who want to work with new technology or in jobs usually considered 'men's jobs'. ESF contribution – £198,000.
- South Glamorgan Women's Workshop, which is training 50 women a year in computing and electronics. An integral part of the workshop is social skills training to help the women gain the confidence they need to return to work, and a free nursery.

New guidelines have been published for 1986–88 and the criteria for eligibility are stricter. Britain, which has hitherto benefited from nearly one-third of the Fund, is likely to face some disappointments.

This is a short-list of the sorts of projects which are the priorities in Great Britain in 1986:

- training or wage support for additional jobs for women in occupations in which they are under-represented
- training for migrant workers and members of their families
- training and work-place adaptations for people with handicaps
- training of development agents for projects in favour of the employment of women, migrant workers and people with handicaps (a migrant worker is not the same as an 'immigrant' as defined by the Home Office)

The projects listed below have priority in the following counties and Scottish regions: Central Cheshire • Cleveland • Clwyd • Cornwall • Derbyshire • Dumfries and Galloway • Durham • Dyfed • Fife • Greater Manchester • Gwent • Gwynedd • Hereford and Worcester • Highlands • Humberside • Isle of Wight • Lancashire • Lincolnshire • Lothian • Merseyside • Mid-Glamorgan • Northumberland • Nottinghamshire • Salop • South Glamorgan • South Yorkshire • Staffordshire • Strathclyde • Tayside • Tyne and Wear • West Glamorgan • West Midlands • West Yorkshire; and travel to work areas: Workington • Coalville • Corby

- training for people over 25 who have been out of work for more than a year
- training or wage support for additional jobs for employment projects run by local groups
- training or wage support for people with disabilities capable of working in the open labour market

Projects which are innovatory can apply for assistance from a special budget within the Social Fund.

Projects in Northern Ireland where special regulations apply should contact the Department of Economic Development or the Department of Employment for full details.

There are some important points to note about the Social

Fund. Grants are only paid for running expenses, including ancillary expenses such as crèche facilities. Grants have to be matched pound for pound by support from local or central government. Applications can generally only be made for operations carried out within one calendar year. In practice this means that only groups with strong support from their source of matching money can risk applying for Social Fund grants.

For details of current guidelines, priorities, timetables and procedures for applications contact the Department of Employment, Overseas Division (OB2), Caxton House, Tothill Street, London SW1B 9NA, or Bill Seary, Head of International Affairs, NCVO, 26 Bedford Square, London WC1B 3HU.

Programme to Combat Poverty

The EEC Programme to Combat Poverty is a fund to finance action-research and innovatory projects which attempt to combat poverty. There are no funds available before 1988 at the earliest. Projects which have been funded were for the benefit of long-term and young unemployed people, elderly people, single parent families, second generation migrants, refugees and returning migrants. If you think you might stand a chance in a new round of funding – if any – after 1988 write to the DHSS or to its equivalent departments in Wales, Scotland or Northern Ireland some time in 1987 for details.

Keep your ears to the ground about other possible sources of EEC funding which are announced from time to time.

5
The Major Non-Statutory Sources of Funding

There are other sources of funds which are nothing to do with the different branches of government. Some might be grant-making bodies, others might be fund-raising activities which you organise. This chapter looks at these non-statutory sources.

GRANT-MAKING TRUSTS

There are about 2,500 grant-making trusts in Britain which each make grants averaging over £1,500 a year. Some have an annual budget running into several millions. This section deals with two major concerns: how trusts operate, and which ones you should approach.

How trusts operate
They are often set up by rich individuals. Some, like the Royal Jubilee Trusts, have been founded by public subscription. Most trusts have a capital fund which is invested to produce an income. It is this investment income from which grants are made.

A trust is run by a group of people known as trustees whose job it is

- to manage the money invested, usually in stocks, shares or property, to produce income
- to make grants to charities or to support the charitable work of

other voluntary organisations in response to applications and appeals received by the trustees

The larger trusts usually employ one or more people to handle the day-to-day work of the trust. These people (known variously as the director, secretary, clerk or administrator) deal directly with the applicants and make recommendations on which applications to support for the trustees to consider and decide on at their trustees' meetings. Who has most influence – the trust secretary or the trustees – depends on the trust. In some trusts the decisions are made entirely by the trustees; in others they in effect rubber-stamp the recommendations of the trust secretary. The day-to-day work of managing the investments is usually undertaken by a stockbroker, bank or the Official Custodian for Charities.

The trustees are not free to make any grant they want. A number of criteria will influence them.

The trust's objects. The objects of charitable trusts can provide a fascinating insight into the social and economic life of a society. Philanthropy is not the sole motivation of many of the wealthy people who devote part of their riches to charity. Money is power in the voluntary sector as much as in business or politics and the 'strings' attached in different ways to charitable giving can often reveal the desires of donors to create the world they value. So, for instance, the objects of a trust, laid down in the constitution, can be very specific. Grants may only be made, say, to promote missionary work overseas, to provide comfort and care for the welfare of four-legged animals in old age, or to send the sons of war widows to school. Assumptions about the role of women in society can often be detected in trusts' objects. There are still many charities, for example, whose objects are the alleviation of distress and poverty among women.

A trust cannot change its objects so long as they are capable of being fulfilled, but when it is no longer possible to do this, the trustees can apply to the courts to have the objects changed.

The trust's policies. Within the trust's permitted objects the trustees may make their own policies of what they will and will not support. Some may have no consistent policies and simply assess each application on its merits. Some trusts produce statements of policy and guidelines for applicants. With others it can be impossible to find out what are the criteria by which they judge applications.

The beneficial area. There may be a geographical area to which the trustees have to restrict their donations.

Status of the applicant. Many trusts will support registered charities only (see Charitable Status, page 39).

Attitudes of trustees. Trustees of grant-making trusts tend to be white, male and middle-aged to elderly. Women are sometimes asked to become trustees but they are almost always in a minority. Trusts are under no obligation to ensure that the trustees are representative of society at large so the opinions and attitudes of any one group of trustees may not be very diverse: the trustees may well hold similar beliefs on the basis of similar experiences of life; they may very well have limited knowledge or understanding of what life is like for many women and may not attach much importance to the issues which concern women. This can be a serious drawback for women's voluntary organisations. The job of winning over such trustees can be difficult. It may be unfair, but it is sensible to be prepared with well-rehearsed arguments and a sure belief in the value of your work.

Some trusts are radical, pioneering and innovative and will be interested in what you are doing. Many take their responsibilities very seriously and understand that they have a duty to contribute to the improvement of society and the relief of deprivation. Good works are broadly what they are interested in so you do have a lot to offer to many trusts. The Allen Lane Foundation, for example, is concerned with the problems of deprivation and handicap and have funded rape crisis centres and women's aid groups. The trustees are aware of the needs of particular groups of girls and women, such as isolated young mothers from ethnic minority communities. They also prefer that youth groups they help have a strong programme for girls.

The Charity Commission recognised the promotion of 'good race relations' as a legal charitable purpose in December 1983. This might help black women's groups to become registered charities, which will increase the chances of getting grants from all sorts of donors, not just charitable trusts. Some grant-making trusts have adopted policies of supporting projects which work towards better race relations or which reflect the needs of ethnic minority communities. The Gulbenkian Foundation gives priority to ethnic minority arts and, as part of its social welfare programme, to ethnic minority groups in general. The King George's Jubilee Trust is also concerned with the needs of ethnic minorities. These are two examples of trusts with explicit policies on funding ethnic minority projects. There are many more trusts that do support such work.

Which trusts to approach

The great majority of trusts will

not be interested in supporting you. They may already have committed all their funds to other causes. Their objects and policies may be completely different from yours. You might not be eligible for other reasons. But there will be some who will consider supporting you.

A major difficulty in knowing which trusts to approach is that very few produce regular reports about their grant-making policies or supply information about themselves beyond the minimum required by the Charity Commission and the Inland Revenue.

Generally, appeals to the very small trusts are pointless because they tend to make donations to particular 'pet' causes. But if you have some personal contact with a trustee you might have a chance.

There are two basic guides to trusts which will give you enough information to plan your approach.

- *The Directory of Grant-Making Trusts* (Charities Aid Foundation, 1985) gives details of about 2,500 trusts. Most trusts with incomes over £1,500 are included and the details given are of the trust's objects, policies, the sorts of grants that are made and who to apply to. There are nine major classifications of charitable purposes: Medicine and Health, Welfare, Education, Sciences, Humanities, Religion, Environmental Resources, International and General. There may be no obvious sources of funding for women, but much of the work of women's voluntary groups fits into these kinds of categories. You can usually find a copy in your local reference library.
- *A Guide to the Major Grant-Making Trusts* (Directory of Social Change, 1986) gives much more detail on the 200 largest trusts which together represent about 80–90 per cent of the total grant income available from trusts.

Other possible sources of information are your local council for voluntary service, the social services department, or, in some areas, a local charities information bureau (see appendix 1, page 116).

What you have to do next is pretty daunting, but take a deep breath and get on with it if you feel you might well need donations from charitable trusts.

You have to compile your own list of trusts to approach. Go through the directories and eliminate the trusts which clearly will be unable to donate money to you for one reason or another. The small number you are left with, which may run to a few hundred, needs to be pruned too. Pick out the ones which might be interested in you because you are in their beneficial area, or because you have an idea they've supported groups like yours before or because you're doing something which they might find adds a new slant to the work they generally fund. Then do as much research on these trusts as possible. Try to find out their detailed policies. Write for guidance notes if they produce them. Find out what size of grant they favour, then compose an application which fits in with their approach. Try to find out if they have ever funded women's groups before. If they have, contact the women involved. They will almost certainly be supportive, and give you useful advice.

You can still contact the ones which seemed less likely to be interested. If you can afford it, send out a circular letter, 'top and tail' it to give it a semblance of uniqueness by typing in the name and address of each trust and signing each letter individually. 'Cold mailing' infuriates a lot of trusts, but then they are probably the ones who would have no interest in you anyway. But there may be the odd one or two who understand that sometimes cold-mailing is the only thing some voluntary groups can afford or have time for and it can bring in reasonably sized donations.

Your initial approach will be in writing. You can offer to meet them or ask them to come and see what you are doing.

There is no list of trusts pledged to supporting women's organisations, although the next edition of *The Directory of Grant-Making Trusts* will include 'women' as a new category for donations. This would be a great step forward, if only as an aid to consciousness-raising as many trusts are completely unaware of the extent and nature of the voluntary work done by women for women (see Introduction).

COMPANIES

Companies do not give very much in charitable donations, around £75 million a year, compared with £300 million from grant-making trusts and at least as much as this from government. They also tend to be very conservative about who they support and tend to avoid anything with radical implications. So many women's organisations will have to weigh up very carefully whether or not there is any point in approaching companies. However if you are looking for relatively small donations, companies, especially small local ones, can be a useful source of support. Read this section and then make up your mind.

Some companies give nothing at all. They see no reason to. But others give substantial amounts each year. Their donations are normally tax deductible so there are financial advantages for them as well as benefits in terms of public relations. The biggest givers are the largest, most profitable companies which includes the banks, the large oil companies and other major companies as the table below shows.

Top 10 Company Donors (1984)

	£
Marks & Spencer	4.7m
NatWest Bank	1.9m
IBM	1.7m
Barclays Bank	1.7m
BP	1.3m
ICI	1.1m
Unilever	0.8m
Shell UK	0.8m
Hanson Trust	0.8m
Midland Bank	0.7m

Source: *Charity Statistics 1984/85*, Charities Aid Foundation

These companies will on average be giving £2 for each £1,000 of profit they earn. They will be receiving thousands of requests. Except in very special circumstances you would be extremely fortunate to get a donation larger than £2,500, and for many companies the amounts they will give will be very much smaller than this, perhaps only £50.

Cash donations are not the only way in which companies can give their support. Companies can and do give away all sorts of things: a gift voucher or some of their products for a raffle, old office furniture or surplus equipment. It's often a lot easier for them to do this than give away money. But don't be afraid of saying 'no thanks' if they offer you a gift in kind which is more likely to be a hindrance than a help, like a clapped out old typewriter.

Telephone or write to the managing director and explain what you would like the company to do. If you're collecting for a raffle or tombola, take a trip down your local high street and ask the shopkeepers for donations. Be sure to tell each one what the others have donated.

Many small businesses can't or won't make donations of any sort, but they might be prepared to contribute in the form of advertising. If you are running an event which needs a programme, or if you're producing a brochure or newsletter, ask people to advertise in it. It's possible to get a lot of firms, shops or self-employed tradespeople to contribute in this way.

Sponsorship has really taken off in recent years. Publicity is the main reward for the company involved and it tends to revolve around sport. Other activities can attract sponsorship but it's a difficult and time-consuming way to win support. But try it. You never know your luck. One charitable organisation has found sponsors for all its overheads from a computer terminal, courtesy of Zenith Data, to sandwiches for staff lunches from Marks & Spencer and Sainsbury's.

Companies can also be persuaded to let you use their facilities, ranging from a photocopier to their boardroom for an important meeting.

Who will companies help?

Most firms do not have a policy as such on which groups they're prepared to help. But most probably make decisions on the basis of the following factors:

- Personal contact. This is probably the single most important factor in being successful in raising money from industry. If the person approaching a company is known to the chairwoman or chairman or to the managing director, not only is it difficult to refuse a request for money, but the size of donation is likely to be respectable. Another strategy is to get a prominent local businessperson to sign your appeal letters. The personal interests of businesspeople also influence their giving. A director of Bovis (the construction company) for instance, became interested in women's refuges and donated a house to Chiswick Women's Aid.
- Playing safe. If what they hope to get out of supporting voluntary activity is good public relations, then companies are going to shy away from anything controversial, 'political' or associated with an unpopular cause. However, if you work out your arguments well in advance and present your case in terms of, say, community development, you may be successful.
- Fashions. At the time of writing (early 1986) industry feels it should be doing something to help mitigate the effects of unemployment, so projects working in this area may find it easier to win support than others. In a few years' time the fashionable cause might be something else.

But there may also be an obvious reason why a company might help.

- A 'product' link where what you are doing somehow relates to the work of the company, such as a Women in Manual Trades course and a builders merchants.
- A 'geographic link' where your work is located in the town where the company has its head office or a large factory. Boots, for example, provides a lot of help to Nottingham charities as its head office is there.
- An 'employment' link. Some companies agree to support charities which their employees work for as volunteers.
- A 'local' touch. Some big firms make donations from the head

office but also make some money available for dispersal through local branches.

What should you do then? As a women's group you face the perennial disadvantage in that so many potential donors do not see the need for special treatment for women. Anything which is vaguely 'feminist' or women-only they find hard to accept. But it is possible to make out a case, even if it means playing down the 'women' angle and playing up something else. The relative success of some women's aid refuges in winning support from all sorts of sources is partly to do with the effects domestic violence has on children, for example. Obviously, it would be wrong to misrepresent oneself, and to deny that women's needs are the motivating priority would be unacceptable, but take a long hard look at your activities and see if there is anything about them which could tie in with the concerns of different companies.

Make a list of all the companies where you have some personal contact and ask for a donation.

Make a shopping list of all the goods and services you need; identify the firms which might be in a position to supply these and approach them. If you do have to buy things ask your supplier for a discount.

Look at what fund-raising events and publicity material you're planning and see if there are any opportunities for donations in kind, sponsorship or advertising.

Who are the prominent businessmen and women in your area? Which large national companies have significant presences in your area? Which are the leading local firms? Which companies need to maintain a good image with the local population? Approach them all.

Make a list of businesses owned and run by women. Think about how best to approach them for support.

You should be able to find out who and where the companies are by looking in the Yellow Pages, or your local paper's advertising pages. Try the local chambers of trade and commerce. The *Times 1,000*, a guide to leading companies in Britain and overseas, gives information on national companies. It should be available in your local library.

Approaches should be made to named individuals, by telephone, followed by a letter. This will ensure you are approaching the right person in the first place. If the switchboard operator can't help, ask for the chairwoman/ chairman or managing director and they will either sort it out or put you on to the right person. Present your case well by avoiding jargon, getting to the point quickly, not being apologetic, spelling out the practical side of your work and how the company could help. Bear in mind that industry on the whole does not have much knowledge or understanding of voluntary organisations in general, let alone women's organisations. Try to ask for something specific, but be prepared to offer alternatives. If they say no to a cash donation, don't let that be an end to it. Try to impress by pointing out some of your achievements. Be proud of yourselves. Suggest ways in which it might benefit the company if they were to be associated with you. For example, you may be able to offer advice on the setting up of workplace nurseries or carers' groups, or on developing an equal opportunities policy.

Once a useful contact has been made keep in touch. Above all let them know how their help was used. It is essential having won someone over to make them feel involved and appreciated.

OTHER WAYS OF RAISING MONEY

So far we have looked at money available from organisations that can make grants to you. There is tremendous competition for these funds with most donor bodies receiving far more applications than they have the resources to support. Many grant-making bodies want to see evidence of public support, and that chiefly means financial support, before they will be persuaded to follow suit.

In fact, members of the public give a massive amount to good causes each year. Individual giving raises as much as the grants given by government, local government, trusts and companies combined.

It can be hard work, time-consuming and even depressing having to search for money wherever you can find it. But women are experienced in doing this. After all, the voluntary sector is characterised by vigorous fund-raising activities. Coffee-mornings, slide shows, raffles, jumble sales, sponsored walks, sales of work, tombolas, you name it, women have organised it and raised substantial sums of money into the bargain.

It sometimes seems like a lot of effort for little return, but the beauty of it is that when this kind of thing does raise money, it is raised quickly, it is cash, it has no strings attached and it has the additional result of getting your message across and building good will and support.

In the following pages we describe a few ways in which you can raise money without applying for grants.

Getting donations from your supporters

Getting supporters to give you money not only provides you with a useful additional source of funds, it can also help you build a healthier and more successful organisation.

If your support comes entirely from one large grant, it becomes quite easy to lose touch with your community and you become too dependent for your survival on whether that grant continues. Getting support from people, individuals not necessarily working with the group, means you avoid that pitfall and you can mobilise it when you need it. If you need money urgently you can send out a special appeal letter; if you want to lobby your local council, you can ask them to write in support of you.

Start with the obvious people: your management committee or trustees (if you have any), your members, your volunteers, people who write to you expressing support, your local community, the women who stand to benefit from your work. Everyone involved in the group or organisation should take on, at minimum, this aspect of fund raising – reaching individual supporters.

Most people only give when asked. If you do nothing no one will know you need support. When you do ask, you will probably be surprised at how generous people can be.

You will need to think about ways in which people can give support and perhaps have a leaflet available about your work. Give people the opportunity of saying they don't need a receipt, otherwise you should always acknowledge donations with a receipt.

Keep a record of all the donations you receive, on either a card index, a register or a computer file. That way, you can ask donors for support again.

Work out the different ways of giving. The most obvious is to ask for a one-off cash donation by direct personal contact. Start with your own friends, relatives and colleagues at work or in other groups you may be involved in. If you can't make personal contact, then write. If there are a lot of people on your list, a standard letter will do.

You can also ask people to subscribe. Subscriptions from members, friends or supporters can give small organisations in particular a regular, reliable income. By setting fixed levels of subscription you know how much you will be getting and your subscribers will know how much exactly they are expected to give. A lot of groups already do this successfully and have found a lot of goodwill among people with relatively little money, so don't forget lower rates of subscription for unwaged supporters like pensioners, children, students and the unemployed.

All the same, make sure your subscription rate is reasonable and is going to make you a little bit of profit beyond the cost of administering the subscriber's membership.

It's also worth suggesting to supporters that they make a regular donation by banker's order from their bank account to yours. They may hardly miss a fiver a month but it could make all the difference to you. The banker's order gets round the problem of relying on their memory to ensure it gets to you regularly.

Donations from individuals and companies often come as gifts in kind, such as a typewriter or the loan of a minibus for a trip. If a firm has its own printing equipment ask for help with producing your annual report. You can ask for skills as well as things: an hour a week of a bookkeeper's time, volunteers to help distribute leaflets in the neighbourhood, a local journalist to write your press releases. Get everyone to sit down and put together a 'wish-list' of everything they need and see if there are ways of circulating the list to the people who might be in a position to help.

If you think your organisation is going to put down roots and will still be thriving in the next century, it may be appropriate for your group to encourage supporters to remember you in their wills. About one-third of the total given to charity in Britain is given in the form of bequests. The National Trust and the RSPCA both recently received a legacy of several million pounds completely out of the blue in this way. Some women's groups, such as those working with carers, may find this an appropriate source of support.

Giving by covenant

If you are a registered charity, you should consider asking supporters to make their donations by covenant. A covenant is a document by which a supporter agrees to give something every year for more than three years. If the supporter pays income tax in the UK, the recipient charity is then able to reclaim the basic rate tax already paid by the supporter on the money s/he earned to make the donation.

If a donor who is a taxpayer decides to give £7 a year by covenant, the charity will be able to reclaim £3 from the Inland Revenue. If the sum given is £10, then the amount of tax reclaimable is £4.28. Thus, giving by covenant increases the value of a donation by 42.8 per cent.

If you like the idea and you're eligible you should have the necessary documents printed. This will normally include a deed of covenant and a banker's order. The deed of covenant is a legal document, so it is important that it is worded properly. You may be able to get a sympathetic solicitor to do this for you. Try your local law centre, women's legal action group, or even the law school at your nearest university or polytechnic.

You then have to reclaim the tax from the Inland Revenue. This means filling in forms obtainable from them. If you have 20 or more covenants, you may find it worthwhile to have the job done for you by Charities Aid Foundation who provide a service which is not too expensive. Details are available from CAF, 48 Pembury Road, Tonbridge, Kent TN9 2JD, tel. 0732-356323.

The following table shows the kind of benefit you would receive from persuading supporters to covenant their donations:

If a supporter gives each year	You get	Total over 4 years
£ 5	£ 7.14	£ 28.56
£10	£14.28	£ 57.12
£25	£35.71	£142.84
£50	£71.42	£285.68

Prepare a basic leaflet

You should produce a simple leaflet about the work of your organisation or group. This can then be:

- sent out with every letter and other communications like newsletters
- left lying around the office, at meetings, conferences, workshops, on stalls and bookstalls
- sent to members of other organisations by agreement with those organisations

The leaflet should be inexpensive to produce, attractive and easy to read, and should contain all the basic information you feel will convince people to support you.

You should include:

- information about the aims of your group, what its work is and why it is important
- information on ways of giving, such as donations, banker's orders, covenants, subscriptions, volunteers
- some form of reply coupon where people can give their name, address and telephone number if you need it, with boxes to tick for the kind of help they are giving, requests for more information, on covenants for instance, and a yes/no box for a receipt if you want to save money on postage

Some thought needs to be put into the design of the leaflet and there are ways of getting help with this without spending a fortune:

- Collect leaflets from the big charities. They all employ professional help and you can get ideas from their literature.
- Contact a local advertising or design agency. They may be prepared to take you on as a charity client.
- Some individual designers, or student designers, are prepared to do work at cost only for voluntary organisations.

The following is an example of a

79

How to Go About It

leaflet produced by the Pankhurst Trust for its Brick Appeal.

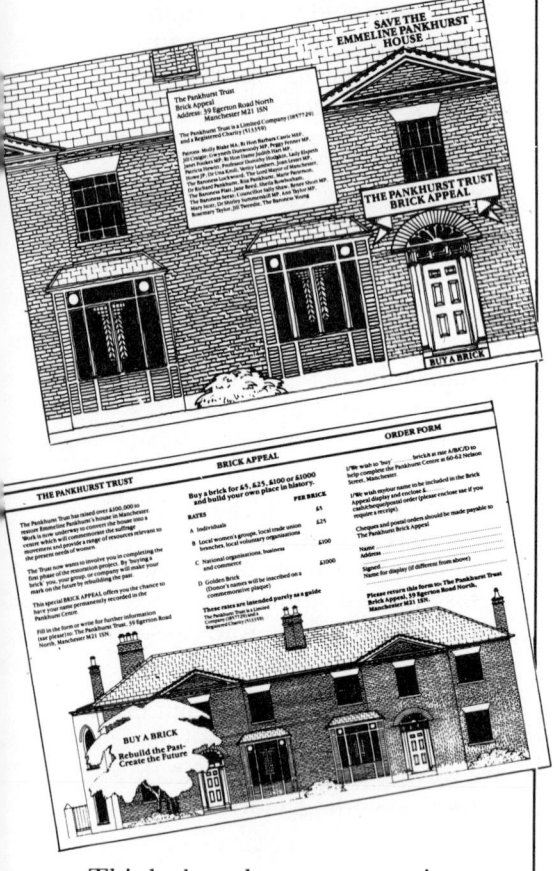

Think about how you are going to distribute the leaflet before you decide how many to print. Bear in mind also that it might become dated in a year or two.

Collections

Charities and other good causes are in a privileged position. They are permitted to collect from the public in various ways provided they keep within the law.

Collecting from the public widens your fund-raising base beyond your committed supporters. People like supporting good causes, they are used to being asked and are generous. You may be able to collect anything from a few hundred pounds upwards from collections. Collections are also an extremely good way of making your presence felt locally and of finding out how much your work is valued by the community.

The main types of collection are:

- street collections or flag days
- house-to-house collections
- pub collections
- carol singing
- whip-rounds at events
- collections of items like foreign coins, old newspapers, etc. which you can then turn into cash
- collecting boxes left in shops, pubs, etc.

To run a street collection, flag day or house-to-house collection you need a permit and you have to comply with a strict set of regulations designed to protect the public, but don't let this put you off. The procedure is actually quite simple. You obtain a permit from your local district council (in London, from the Metropolitan Police). For pub collections you also need the landlord's consent at each pub.

Collections on private premises are not subject to regulations although they must be conducted with the permission of the owner of the premises. It is not generally realised how extensive the opportunities for collecting on private premises are. Cinemas and theatres, for example, are areas where such collections can take place.

You need collecting boxes which you can sometimes borrow from other, large organisations. Your local council for voluntary service may be able to help here. You also need volunteers. They are not usually hard to find if you ask around widely enough. People who may not want to get involved in a committed way may be happy to devote a day or part of a day to raising money for you in this way.

You can also organise impromptu whip-rounds at events, whether directly connected with your group, such as an open meeting, or even your own private parties. Guests at a party a few years ago were a bit taken aback half way through the evening to be asked to cough up for a women's health project in Zimbabwe, but they did all the same. They put it down to eccentricity and £50 was collected.

Events and activities

When you are thinking of organising special events, it is important to think it through before you make your first move.

What are you planning? Who is going to come? How are you going to sell tickets or advertise the event? How much money will it involve? Are you sure to make a profit? Is it really a promotional event rather than a fund-raising event? What are you budgeting for it? Have you got the organisational capacity to pull it off successfully?

Every group and organisation should organise at least one event each year. It serves several purposes. It can be a social event, it can raise money, it can get publicity, it can attract new members, it can promote good community relations, it can reinforce your own solidarity and a spirit of sisterhood.

Try to follow some basic rules. Reduce the possibility of making a financial loss as far as you can. Plan well ahead to avoid last minute panics and disasters. Learn from experience so that you can do the same thing next year with enhanced results. Build in other fund-raising activities. For instance, if you are organising a disco, make sure everyone gets a leaflet when they leave, or run a tombola at your jumble sale. Sell drinks at different points on your sponsored walk. Use well-known personalities if it's appropriate. They're crowd-pullers. Make sure you get a mention in the local media. Go for an event which will give people pleasure and fun. People respond more enthusiastically if they know their time and money is going to be spent enjoyably.

Sponsorship. Most people have been asked at some time or another to sponsor a friend, colleague or relative in some sort of fund-raising activity, such as running a marathon, knitting squares, swimming, walking or whatever. The main drawback is the difficulty in collecting the money. But sponsorship of this type is a worthwhile fund-raising technique. People give to support their friends as well as to support the cause. It's hard to say no. Virtually any group or organisation has the potential to raise a four-figure sum in this way.

You need to supply sponsorship forms and explanatory literature about your organisation. And most important of all, you need to put pressure on the participants to collect the money from their sponsors and hand it over to you.

Lotteries and raffles. Lotteries, including raffles, sweepstakes, grand draws, tombolas and other amusements with an entry fee and prizes are run by many organisations to raise money. Lotteries are regulated by the 1976 Lotteries and Amusements Act and can be run by any charity or good cause organisation. The regulations specify the size of the lottery, how much can be distributed as prizes and used to cover expenses, and how the lottery should be run. A lottery must be registered with the district or borough council who will have details of the requirements.

A sweepstake is a lottery the result of which is determined by the outcome of a horse race such as the Derby or the Grand National. Most offices organise sweepstakes for at least the Grand National. Get your members to organise one at their place of work or amongst their friends and split the takings between your own funds and the prize for the winner.

Tombolas are familiar fixtures at church sales, summer fairs, village fêtes, etc. They're great fun. Most prizes are donated and are allocated a ticket with a number. For a small entry fee, say 10p or 6 for 50p, the participant draws a ticket which may or may not have a number corresponding with a prize. There's often a compulsion to try again if you don't win first time. The secret, if you're organising a tombola, is to have a number of 'star prizes' (for some reason they're usually alcoholic), and to keep the tickets out of the pool until near the end. You should also work out a fair proportion of numbered tickets to unnumbered. Children particularly like tombolas, so make sure you have prizes that will please them as well as adults (although they are often thrilled to be able to present their prize to Mum or Dad).

Advertising. Anything you print can carry advertising. The money you get can help cover the printing costs and even contribute to the costs of the group. Advertising is a useful way of getting money out of smaller companies, even the corner shop, as it is a tax deductible expense. It is convenient and at least it generates good will towards the business to be seen to be supporting a charitable or other voluntary organisation.

What are you producing which could carry advertising? It could be a regular newsletter, annual report, wall chart, year planner or pamphlet. Would advertising be out of place in it? Do you have any objections in principle to advertising?

For example, say you have to produce an annual report and it's going to cost £200. Ask eight local companies or small businesses to sponsor it by contributing £25 each. Or find eight women who make their living by selling their skills, such as carpenters or electricians, to do the same. Then at the front or on the back page, mention the fact that the report has been sponsored by them.

When you're thinking of using advertising in this way, try to get a few initial commitments before taking the plunge. It helps to persuade others if you can say 'so-and-so's already agreed'. Produce a covering letter which sets out your plans and date of publication, the circulation, the rates you are charging and the deadline for copy. One problem can be artwork. Many smaller businesses don't have standard advertisements ready designed. See if you can get a volunteer to fill this gap for you so you can offer it as an extra service to the advertisers. You could even levy a small charge.

Make sure you get the money!

Using the media

There are all sorts of ways in which the media can help you, even though the images of women and the racism in the media are often infuriating.

Radio and television appeals. Each week on Radio 4 on a Sunday morning there is an appeal to raise money for a particular charity. Once a month on both ITV and BBC television appeals are broadcast. In Scotland, Wales and Northern Ireland some local appeals are broadcast for charities in those parts of the UK only. These appeals can raise considerable sums of money. The average is around £10,000 for a national radio appeal, £18,000 for a tv appeal and £1,000 for a Scottish, Welsh or Northern Irish appeal.

All applications are considered by a Central Appeals Advisory Committee and you can apply only once every two years. You should send your applications for BBC slots to the Appeals Assistant, BBC, Broadcasting House, London W1A 1AA, and for ITV

83

slots to the Appeals Secretary, IBA, 70 Brompton Road, London SW3 1EY.

Local newspapers. Try to build a good relationship with your local paper, on a personal basis with reporters if possible. You may be able to interest them in events you organise, or in articles about your work, particularly when you produce annual reports. You may be able to persuade a local journalist to act as a press officer for you, to write press releases and to advise you how to handle the press, what sorts of things the press will be interested in and how to cope with bad publicity, which sometimes happens. If you are receiving substantial amounts of public money, in particular, you must understand that the press are inevitably going to be interested in who you are and what you are doing. Don't be defensive. Be helpful. Invite a journalist along to meet you to discuss your work. Try to anticipate press coverage and prepare your conversation with the reporters who will be contacting you. If necessary ask them if you can ring them back shortly when they phone so you can gather your thoughts. Channel press inquiries to one or two people with a special responsibility for press relations if possible.

There may be specialist newspapers or magazines which may be interested in your work. If you are a black women's group, try the ethnic minority press, if you are working on education issues, what about the *Times Educational Supplement*? And, of course, there are innumerable women's magazines to approach. There are several directories to the press in the UK which are usually available in your local library. Look through them and compile your own press list of publications to contact when you want publicity.

Local radio. Much of the above also applies to your local radio station, both the BBC and commercial stations. It's not just news they're looking for. There are phone-in and advice programmes. If you are working on meeting a particular need or solving a problem this might offer an opportunity for publicity. Offer to participate as a special adviser on the basis of your unique expertise. For instance, if you run a Lesbian Line, find out if there are any sensitive presenters or producers who might be prepared to host a programme highlighting your service and skills.

A few local radio stations also run a radio appeal once a year to raise money for good causes in their area. The largest of these is the Capital Radio 'Help a London Child' appeal which benefits London-based organisations dealing with children. Find out if your own local station has anything on the same lines.

Specialist radio and television programmes. There are several specialist programmes which you should consider in the same way as the specialist publications. For instance, if you are a group working on disability there is 'Does He Take Sugar?' on Radio 4. Why not suggest to Radio 4 that they consider a 'Does She Take Sugar?' slot featuring the special needs and interests of women with disabilities? Channel 4 Television has a policy of showing specialist programmes: there have been programmes for women generally, for older people and for the Afro-Caribbean and Asian communities; there are sports programmes, children's programmes, and other special interest areas which you might be able to fit into. Find out what the specialist programmes are and contact them to see if they might be interested in featuring you. You won't be able to appeal for money, but the publicity will be valuable.

Commercial television contractors. Many of the ITV stations have set up charitable trusts to distribute money to local charities. Granada and Central give money in this way, for example. It's worth contacting the one in your area.

Thames TV and the BBC both run 'Telethons' which raise money from the public to be distributed to applicant charities. The Thames Help Trust and the BBC Children in Need appeal are both aimed at helping children and young people.

Earning and saving money

It is far easier to spend money than to raise it. So it's worthwhile thinking of ways of spending less, hanging on to your money longer, earning money and making savings.

Rates. If you are established as a charity, you will be entitled to receive 50 per cent mandatory rate relief on the premises you occupy. Apply to the Rating Department, and while you're at it ask about discretionary rate relief. While they have to give you mandatory relief, they can decide whether or not to give you relief on the other 50 per cent.

Bank charges and interest. When you choose a bank try to get the following:

- a promise of no bank charges
- automatic transfer of money on current account to interest-bearing deposit account.

If one bank won't do this, try another. Use the influence of prominent supporters. Bank at their branch. For large amounts of money, shop around to find the deposit account which offers the highest rate of interest.

Because you can earn up to 15 per cent per annum interest it is worth making sure your cash balances are as high as possible.

85

Try to:

- Collect any outstanding sums as quickly as possible.
- Ask your funding bodies to pay in advance, in a lump sum and as soon as possible after the start of your financial year. The money could be earning interest in your account, not theirs. This may be impossible to accomplish, but there's no harm in asking.

If you are a charity, you will not have to pay tax on your investment income and where it is received tax paid, you will usually be able to reclaim it from the Inland Revenue.

When you can't get goods and services donated in kind, buy from suppliers who might be prepared to give you a discount. Ask for a discount and explain why you need one. The local authority or education authority may have a Supplies Department which can purchase and resell items to voluntary organisations. Often the prices they can offer are well below anything you could find elsewhere. Find out if your organisation is eligible, who to contact and how to get a price list.

Look at ways in which you might be able to earn money. It may be that you can charge for certain goods and services. Do you sell publications? Are you charging enough? Do you provide speakers for other organisations? Could you charge a small fee? Do you run a café? How much are you making? Do you run an evening class? Do you hold workshops or training sessions? Obviously you must draw the line at your voluntary work which is done for other poeple's benefit free of charge. But if it's clear that other organisations or agencies consistently come to you because of your expertise in a particular field, then perhaps it's time to start charging them.

Volunteers

Are you short-handed? Do you need particular skills which are not available in the group or among existing staff? Would you be able and willing to use volunteers to fill the gap? If so, here are some tips on how to find them.

- A local volunteer bureau may be channelling volunteers to local organisations. Look in the telephone book for your local council for voluntary service who would know.
- Local and national radio and TV may be broadcasting appeals for volunteers. Details are given in the *Directory of Social Action Programmes*, available from the Volunteer Centre Media Project at 29 Lower King's Road, Berkhamstead, Herts HP4 2AB, tel. 04427-73311.
- The Retired Executives Action Clearing-House (REACH) channels retired people into

voluntary organisations. You go on a register until they find someone to help you. Contact REACH at 89 Southwark Street, London SE1 0HD, tel. 01-928 0452.
- Community Service Volunteers at 237 Pentonville Road, London N1 9NJ, tel. 01-278 6601, operate a

scheme where they place young volunteers with you full time for a few months or longer. You are expected to provide board and lodging and pocket money.
- Your own supporters. Through your newsletter or leaflet you can tell your supporters that you need help and what sort of help you require.

6
Developing Other Sources of Funding

NETWORKING

Mary Seacole returned to London from the Crimean War, famous but penniless. It was 1857 and she was 52 years old. A nurse, she had been born in Jamaica and in the Crimea had been as celebrated as Florence Nightingale. Unlike Florence Nightingale, who is still honoured to the extent that ten pound notes carry her portrait, the black nurse has largely been forgotten. But in 1857 the military men she had helped survive the war now came to her aid. To raise funds for her, a four-day music festival was organised in London's Surrey Gardens, with over a thousand performers, nine military bands and an orchestra.

Mary Seacole would not normally have been a member of the military network which came to her aid. But having shared their experiences and aided them in the Crimea, the network embraced her at the time of her greatest need. It was an example of how personal contact and common interests can lead to 'networking'.

The term may be relatively new but the practice is not. It is as old as human society. The powerful and powerless both depend on networks as the base from which to maintain or increase their power. Through the supportive character of networks, information and skills are exchanged and a sense of identity is forged. The best known example, The Old Boys' Network, needs no introduction. The formal and informal groupings which are a familiar part of male life, whether they are Rotary Clubs, Freemasons' Lodges, professional associations, or simply ties formed by class associations or common schooling, have long been fascinating phenomena for women in search of the sources of male power.

As in the case of Mary Seacole, these male networks do sometimes benefit women. But women are well aware of the double-edged nature of male patronage. This is one reason why women have found it necessary to strengthen their own hand by organising separately from men on issues ranging from winning the vote to working in the manual trades. This chapter attempts to explore ways of translating this need for female solidarity into financial muscle by suggesting ways in which women could develop the sources of financial support which are closest to them.

Women give a great deal of money away. However badly off they may be, women are always ready to put their hands in their purses in response to shopping precinct tin rattlers, door-to-door collections, or newspaper appeals to fill in a coupon and send a donation to a particular national charity. In addition, the voluntary labour women donate to good causes is itself equivalent to an untold fortune: baking, knitting, sewing, tea-making, stall-holding, entertaining, raffle-ticket selling and jumble-collecting. Women are no strangers to the small-scale labour-intensive fund-raising schemes which attract small individual cash contributions totalling relatively large sums of money at the end of the day.

But are women generous enough to each other? Could women help each other more? Women have limited resources, in terms of time and energy, not just cash and facilities. Could these be put to better use? In the difficult times facing women can a new spirit of female philanthropy and self-sufficiency be forged?

There is a famous women's newspaper in India called *Manushi* and the women running it refuse to accept government money. They say that if they can't survive on financial support from women, then they are not doing their job properly. Women in many other countries have strong views on this point as well. In Holland, many women's groups have a policy of not taking funds from statutory sources. In Britain, one woman fund raising for a long-running feminist organisation commented:

American women are staggered at how little money British feminists have and wonder whether British feminists are poor or just mean. It's probably a bit of both, but women from other countries, such as Italy,

think that in a country which is relatively well off such as ours, the women's movement should be able to fund itself.

For a variety of reasons, we are probably a long way off being in this position of complete self-sufficiency, desirable though it may be to many. But there are steps which could be taken to strengthen women's financial independence and increase their mutual support of each other. It already happens to some extent. Many Housewives Register branches adopt a 'charitable cause' to fund raise for each year and they are often women's refuges. Many of the older established women's organisations like the Soroptomists have similar policies. This chapter offers some suggestions on how this approach can be extended and made more deliberate as a survival strategy for women in the years to come.

WHO TO APPROACH

People's lives are made up of diverse interests and it is very common for people to be members of more than one group, whether it is a formal organisation or an informal network of friends, relatives, neighbours, church congregations or colleagues. The techniques of the telephone tree, pyramid selling and chain letters are all dependent on this. In 1985,

an ad hoc group called Mothers United was formed very rapidly through such networks and raised £10 a head to pay for a national newspaper advertisement expressing opposition to Victoria Gillick's campaign on contraception and the under-16s.

Let's take an example of how a woman might fit into such networks. This woman has a job. She will be a member of the workforce and she may belong to the relevant trade union. There may be a social club at work which she could belong to, or a women's group. She may have a small child which may have brought her in contact with other mothers near her home. Perhaps they co-operate in a baby-sitting circle, or meet regularly for a night out. She may be a member of a political party or a darts team at the local pub. And if she has any time to spare, she may be a member of your voluntary organisation.

There are several ways in which your colleague could help your fund-raising effort. She could talk to all the different people she has contact with about the voluntary work she does and give out a few leaflets. She might even be able to persuade other women to join you, if you need new members. She could get her workmates, the people in her union and party branch, the regulars at the pub and her women friends to sponsor her in a sponsored walk. She could get the social club to make a donation from its charity fund and ask the landlord or landlady at the pub to donate a bottle of whisky for the tombola at your jumble sale. There are lots of other possibilities.

The point is that you can build a network of support, not just for the group itself, but for the individual members of it. Other groups and organisations which identify with your work and would be prepared and able to support you will be few. Formal approaches on a wider scale may bring a negative or even hostile response, especially if what you are doing is new and people are unfamiliar with the problem. On hearing about it out of the blue, their first reaction might be: 'I don't agree with that.' But if they can identify the group's work with someone they know, like this woman, then they might see it in a totally different light and be prepared to make a contribution. So don't be defensive. Your task is not only to raise funds but to change public opinion about the problem you are concerned with. People's personal respect or affection for you will affect their opinions of the issue. They may still not agree with you, but they will probably end up seeing your point and helping you out if they can.

Here are some ideas about who to approach.

Women's Organisations

Other women's organisations may be struggling with similar problems to your own. They may not as organisations have the resources to support other enterprises. But some may well make a point of fund raising for other causes, and individual members may be prepared to make a contribution to help you out. If that is so, it is up to you to assess which of them to approach. As with other bodies, particularly charitable trusts, you should be prepared to make a good case. You should not assume that just because an organisation is a *woman's* organisation, that they will automatically react in your favour when approached. Women are not a monolithic group with one set of opinions and concerns in common. That much is clear from the complexities of an issue like abortion. Women are an extremely diverse and very large group. So choose with care when you are considering appealing to other women for help. Look for the points of interest you do share so that you develop a sense of partnership.

No one body systematically monitors all national and local women's organisations. Nor has any research been done into whether they are willing and able to help other groups. Again, there is no blueprint for success if you decide to try this approach. You will have to do the research yourself to find out which groups there are in the first place and then which groups to approach. There are several federations of women's organisations and there are some institutions which produce directories of women's organisations. Others keep records for their own purposes, like mailing lists.

Women's organisations cover practically every aspect of life in Britain today. Some are mass membership organisations with a long and venerable history such as the Townswomen's Guild or the International Alliance of Women. Others are much smaller groups working on feminist campaigns which have grown out of the most immediate realities affecting women's lives today, whether the threat of deportation to Asian women and their children or the restriction of choice in childbirth. Women's pressure groups, support groups and caucuses have also been established in many trades, professions and types of work from banking to brick-laying and in all manner of institutions from trade unions to universities. Wherever women are present in significant numbers there is likely to be a women's network of one description or another.

The Women's National Commission is a government advisory committee. It publishes a list of women's organisations in Great Britain which contains separate sections on Scotland and Wales and on organisations concerned with pregnancy, children and families. It includes organisations which promote the interests and welfare of women, professional organisations, religious bodies, women's sections of political parties and a number of international bodies whose headquarters are in Britain. With a few exceptions, local bodies are not included. It contains 165 entries and each one gives the full name, address and telephone number, the main contact person, the founding date, membership, any publications and the group's objects. The total membership of those listing individual members runs into several millions.

There is not the space in this book to include the full list, which you can get free from the Women's National Commission, Government Offices, Great George Street, London SW1P 3AQ. But to give you an idea of the range of organisations included, here is a brief selection:

Academic Women's Achievement Group
Association of British Paediatric Nurses
Association of Women Solicitors
British Women Pilot's Association
Cinema of Women
Equal Pay and Opportunity Campaign
Hysterectomy Support Group
International Toastmistress Clubs
League of Jewish Women
National Advisory Centre on Careers for Women

National Association of Widows
National British Women's Total
  Abstinence Union
National Organisation for
  Women's Management
  Education
Rights of Women
Sangam – Association of Asian
  Women
Suffragette Fellowship
United Kingdom Federation of
  Business and Professional
  Women
Women in Medicine
Women's Advertising Club of
  London
Women's National Cancer Control
  Campaign
Young Women's Christian
  Association of Great Britain

Organisations in Scotland and Wales
Church of Scotland Women's
  Guild
Scottish Convention of Women
Scottish Society of Women Artists
Wales Assembly of Women
Welsh Women's Aid

*Organisations concerned with
pregnancy, children and families*
Association for Improvements in
  the Maternity Services
British Organisation of
  Non-Parents
Family Forum
Foundation for the Study of Infant
  Deaths – Cot Death Research
  and Support
Miscarriage Association
National Childminding
  Association

National Council for Carers and
  their Elderly Dependants
Pre-School Playgroups Association

Other bodies which might be able to help you identify sympathetic women's organisations are NCVO, particularly its Women's Organisations Interest Group, the Equal Opportunities Commission, your local council for voluntary service, the Women's Committee or Equal Opportunities Committee of your local council if it has one, your local Community Relations Council, your local Women's Centre, Resource Centre or Law Centre if there are any in your area. The Spare Rib Diary has a good listings section and there are several federations and associations of women's organisations. You might be affiliated to some already. Start with the ones your own members know about and work from there. The Councils for Voluntary Service – National Association is committed to developing its work with women's organisations and this might be another way in to different women's networks (see appendix 1).

Trade Unions and Political Parties

The trade unions and political parties are mixed organisations with mass membership, but they also have structures and policies relevant to women. You might have members of the different unions and parties in your own ranks.

You will almost certainly have contact at some time with politicians at local level at least, when you are lobbying in support of a grant application. Asking for support from their party organisations does not necessarily imply party political affiliations. After all, political parties are voluntary organisations too and as such they are likely to share your concerns about local conditions. You may not agree with each other in all things, but there may be some aspects of their policies which directly relate to your objectives. If you want to avoid even the remotest possibility of appearing politically biased, you could always approach *all* of the parties and let them know that that is what you are doing. Rather than risk unnecessary controversy, time your approaches carefully. Avoid the run up to elections and the period before and after grant applications, especially to local councils, are dealt with.

Trade unions are used to receiving appeals for financial assistance from a variety of groups. The remarkable fund-raising effort during the 1984/85 Miners' Strike is evidence of the resources the Labour Movement is able to draw on. Much less dramatic causes are discussed at meetings up and down the country all the time and modest contributions are made with regularity. However, trade unions are not geared up to function as grant-making bodies. While they are unable to fill the gaps left after abolition, they could be persuaded to support work like your own more systematically than they do at present. It is up to you to approach them systematically. See chapters 3 and 7 for guidance on applying for funding.

Most requests to unions for financial assistance are dealt with on an ad hoc basis. Applications are assessed on merit. It is unlikely that a union will have a policy on who or what to support. But some unions, especially those with a large female membership, have Women's Officers and/or special committees to represent women members, and they have policies on women which have been adopted as a result of the demands of the women members. These are the ones which may be most responsive to an approach from your group. Among the most important in this respect are:

Transport and General Workers Union
General Municipal Boilermakers and Allied Trades Union
National and Local Government Officers Association
National Union of Public Employees
Confederation of Health Service Employees
Union of Shop Distributive and Allied Trades
AUEW-TASS

Society of Civil and Public Servants
Civil and Public Servants Association
National Union of Tailors and Garment Workers
Association of Scientific Technical and Managerial Staffs
Banking Insurance and Finance Union
National Union of Teachers
Association of Professional Executive Clerical and Computer Staffs

How you approach them is important. You could write to the general secretary who will probably pass your letter to the women's officer, if there is one, for an opinion. The general secretary may then take a decision or it could be dealt with by the National Executive Committee or the Finance and General Purposes Sub-Committee. Another approach is to start at the bottom, and develop contact with the local branches and through them the regional organisation. It might be an idea to get to know women in the union first so that you have some support to rely on when your request is being considered.

Trades Councils are the district organisations of the Trades Union Congress (TUC) which also has a regional forum. They often consider appeals for help and are usually interested in hearing speakers. They themselves are networks of trade unions and contacts there can be very useful. You should be able to get details of the Trades Council and Regional TUC for your area from the TUC, Congress House, Great Russell Street, London WC1B 3LS, tel. 01-636 4030.

The best guide to trade unions is *The Trade Union Directory: A Guide to All TUC Unions* by Jack Eaton and Colin Gill, published by Pluto Press, The Works, 105a Torriano Avenue, London NW5 2RX, tel. 01-481 1973.

Industry and Commerce

As we have seen, donations made by private firms to charitable causes are not extensive. But you might be able to do more to encourage and persuade businesspeople to support you. Start by making a list of all the firms where your members in employment work. Find out which companies are the main sources of employment for women generally in your area and which ones rely on women as customers for their goods and services. A fairly recent development has been the tendency of the major companies to describe themselves as 'equal opportunity' employers. Keep an eye out for job advertisements which say this and add the firm's name to your list. If you are successful in your approach to a trade union, ask them which firms their members work for and whether the firms would be worth contacting. If your relationship

95

with the trade union is particularly good you could even ask them to do it on your behalf. Many firms have a public relations department or a 'social affairs' department. They should be told about your work. Some companies like to be seen to be doing 'good works': it's good for their image and for consumer and industrial relations.

Industry and commerce might be the most difficult area for women to develop networks in but it is in the nature of networks that once you are in you stand to gain considerably. People follow fashions, jump on bandwagons, don't like to be left out or to appear out of touch with modern trends. Word gets round about who's doing what for whom and everyone wants to follow suit. The phenomenon of the 'equal opportunity employer', for instance, was unheard of 10 years ago but now it is all the rage. You might be able to use this as an argument in your favour.

Industry and commerce have their own networks of course: trade associations, employers associations, the Confederation of British Industry, the Institute of Directors, and Chambers of Trade and Commerce. Engineering employers, for instance, have developed close links with the Equal Opportunities Commission. They might understand the need for, say, information packs on engineering for girls, and be prepared to support a voluntary project. The climate of opinion about women had moved sufficiently far by November 1985 for the Institute of Directors to hold its first ever conference on why so few women reach the top in business and the professions. It pays to keep the pressure up when this kind of thing starts to happen. Think creatively along those lines. You never know your luck.

Men's Networks

There are all male organisations like the Round Table Clubs and Lions Clubs which have a strong tradition of supporting good causes. Other predominantly male groups, like football supporters clubs, British Legion clubs, Labour clubs, working men's clubs, professional associations or sports clubs might be worth considering. Even if they discriminate against women in their membership rules (as many affiliates of the Club and Institute Union do), they often maintain a fund-raising effort on behalf of the community at large. There's no harm in asking for a share, or getting the men in your life to make representations on your behalf in their clubs and networks.

Other networks

- Your relatives.
- Students. Student unions house numerous societies and women's groups as well as official student

bodies such as community action groups. Rag weeks, halls of residence, departmental social clubs, post-graduate clubs, careers advisory services, religious groups and chaplaincies are all possibilities.
- Ex-colleagues, old school friends, people who owe you small favours and groups you have helped in the past.
- Your own parties. Hold a whip-round half-way through. Leave a pile of leaflets in the hall.
- Shops, markets, supermarkets or launderettes where you are a regular customer. Ask if you can put up a poster.
- Your local community centre, sports centre, village hall or parish rooms and the other groups which use the same premises.
- Your local Member of Parliament is a member of a very important network. Is there anything he or she can do for you?
- Sister organisations abroad. Can you develop close ties with groups in other countries working along the same lines?
- Community health councils, health centres, hospitals, schools, school governors, parent/teacher associations, chambers of trade and commerce, libraries, and any other locally-based group whose own objectives might match yours in one respect or another.
- Church congregations and church bodies, such as Diocesan organisations.

WHAT TO ASK FOR

There are different ways you can ask for help through the various networks you develop contact with. If a particular organisation has a national structure, approach your local branch first.

- You could ask for a straight donation from the branch as a whole or you could suggest that individual members are asked to make donations.
- Suggest the branch 'adopts' your group for a year as the community project they put as top priority for their fund-raising activities.
- You could ask them to circulate your leaflet and appeal letter at meetings or to send out your literature with their own mailings. They may even include an appeal on your behalf in their own newsletters and magazines.
- Ask if they would like to exchange speakers.
- Is there any scope for joint fund-raising activities? Doing things in partnership can expand the possibilities for all the participants. A Christmas bazaar where each group has a stall, held on a regular basis, could develop into a significant

fund-raising and promotional event and at the same time give a focus for women's groups in a particular locality.
- If they are the kind of organisation which passes motions ask them to pass one supporting you and calling on individual members to make a contribution.
- Suggest that they persuade the national 'parent' group to support you, too.
- If they organise conferences, ask if you can have a stall or hold a fringe meeting where you can sell literature, hold a collection and hand out membership forms.
- Suggest they affiliate to your organisation. This is a favourite of trade unions. They often prefer to make a contribution to general funds rather than cover the cost of a project or part of a specific salary.
- Other formal networks are usually voluntary organisations like yourselves with their own objectives. See if there is any common ground. The Society of Civil and Public Servants, for instance, adopted a policy of encouraging members of the public to take up their social security benefits. But before they could launch their own campaign they needed some research to be done and so they part-funded a research officer with a voluntary group called Action for Benefits. The Transport and General Workers Union has contributed to the administrative costs of a workplace nursery scheme. The Association of Cinematograph and Television Technicians made a donation to a video on technical jobs in broadcasting which was aimed at schoolgirls and made by a group called New Girls Network.
- The networks may be able to offer practical help such as the use of meeting rooms, office space, administrative assistance, and printing and photocopying facilities.
- Offer your services to other organisations and charge appropriate fees, travelling expenses and subsistence. A group called Women Against Sexual Harassment has provided speakers, workshop leaders, information and consultancy on policy to unions.
- If you produce publications, package your information in different ways for different markets. This will increase your sales at little extra cost.
- Watch out for public statements other organisations make. For instance, companies which say they feel a responsibility for improving the local environment may be persuaded to pay for having the outside of your premises painted.
- Ask your boss to support an application to the groups she/he belongs to or to arrange for you to do a talk at their meetings.

- Ask a likely employer to raise the possibility of 'payroll giving' with their workforce. This is a new idea in Britain and may be hard to organise, but we are going to hear more and more about it. Under this scheme, employees agree to allow their employer to deduct a small amount, such as 10p each week, from their pay. This is then redistributed to a designated charity, community trust or staff charity fund. For advice on payroll giving, contact Derek Lowman, United Funds at NCVO, 26 Bedford Square, London WC1B 3HD, tel. 01-636 4066.

- Ask for volunteers when you need them. It may be for a couple of hours for a street collection or one evening a week to answer telephones. People may have things they could lend you too, such as a car or van to collect or deliver something when you're stuck, or a computer to do your annual accounts.

7
Applying for Funding and Following Up

PRESENTING YOUR CASE

Before you fill in an application form, it is well worthwhile to speak to another women's group or organisation which has already applied, successfully or unsuccessfully, to the donor you are planning to approach. Many donors publish the names of their grant recipients. Otherwise you may be able to find out who has been funded by whom through your own contacts and networks. They will tell you some of the 'do's and don'ts', one of which is that you should try not to duplicate their application too closely.

Potential donors receive thousands of applications and the situation is getting worse as funds shrink and needs grow. The majority of applications received by any one source of support are turned down. This chapter offers some guidance on how to increase your chances by formulating a good application. As we've said, it's up to you to identify the places which you think might support you. The list of possibles will be different for each group, organisation or project. But there are some factors which should be common to all the applications you make and these are dealt with here in turn.

What you are 'selling'

When you apply for grants, in return for the donor's support you

are 'selling' three things:
- the importance of the work you are doing
- the worthiness of your own organisation
- the ability of you and your group to carry out the proposed work

Ask yourself these questions:
- Why on earth should anyone want to support you?
- What is so special about what you are doing?

If you can communicate these points enthusiastically you will have made a good start.

The need

Many applications refer to 'serious problems', 'extremely urgent needs', 'highly important work'. To donors who read these phrases time and time again these applications are unconvincing.

Try to be precise about the need for the work you are doing. Give figures wherever you can, from your own records, or from official literature like government reports or census data (this is particularly important for Urban Programme applications).

Your reputation

If people believe in you it helps enormously. If you've been in existence for some time, try to show that you can deliver, that there are no skeletons in your cupboard, that your organisation runs efficiently, that you're honest and your work is unique. If you are just setting up try to get some media publicity – you're news! Send your statement of aims, if you've agreed one, to councillors and other people you hope to influence.

Understanding the donor

Try to tailor each application to meet the requirements of the donor.

At all times do some basic research beforehand. Find out:

- the correct name and address of the donor body and the correct person to write to
- their procedure for dealing with applications, particularly whether or not they have a standard application form
- their timetables for considering applications
- the approximate size of grant made
- the sort of work they support

Don't send a duplicated mail shot unless you can't find the resources to do anything fancier. Many potential sources of money will have specific application forms and in that case the officers who receive the forms are usually more than willing to discuss your application in advance and to help you fill it in.

101

Hints on letter writing

If a covering letter is required with an application form, or if the application itself is a letter, the points you should cover are:

- Who are you?
- How much do you want?
- How is the money going to be spent?
- Why should they support you?
- When do you need the money?
- Who else are you applying to?
- What are your long-term funding plans?

If the style is readable it's more likely to be read, so you should:

- Be brief. A one or two-page letter is best supported by something like your annual report or a pamphlet if needs be.
- Avoid waffle. If you can't organise your thoughts well on paper they may think you can't organise your project properly either.
- Avoid jargon. Get a friend unconnected with the group to read your application to see if they can understand what you've written.
- Lay it out attractively. Use short sentences and shortish paragraphs. Use headlines and sub-heads to break up the text. Have it typed neatly.
- Set the right tone. Be confident and straightforward. Don't hector, lecture or demand support. And don't beg either.

How much to ask for

Suppose you need £10,000 and you are approaching a trust which has an annual donations programme of £150,000, how much should you ask for? Some possibilities are a donation of a specific amount, say £2,500; a donation to cover the costs of a particular piece of work; a contribution to your overall costs.

The main thing is to give some indication of where else you are looking for money particularly if you are not asking for the full amount. It's a matter for your own judgement as to how much you do ask for on the basis of your research on the donor.

Conditions

Grants almost always have strings attached. At the very least, you either have to supply accounts or a final report. Many of the major donors monitor your work closely and some stipulate very harsh conditions. This is something you should find out about at the outset because there may be conditions which you would find unacceptable.

NCVO has produced a Code to help voluntary organisations hang on to their independence as best they can. It is available from the Organisation Development Department, NCVO, 26 Bedford Square, London WC1B 3HU.

Timing

Getting a grant can take ages. You have your own time-scale for getting things done and the donors have theirs. Keep your eye on deadlines for applications. You may feel that you haven't got the time it takes for a grant application to be processed. But if you do not have the money to do the work, then one way or another the time will have to be found. The main thing is not to panic and not to get despondent. Get a couple of people to do the paper work. Mutual support is the answer to a lot of the problems caused by shortage of time.

FOLLOWING UP

To be efficient, and therefore to increase your chances of success, there are several things you can do once your application has gone out.

Lobby

This can be done fairly discreetly in so far as the donor itself is concerned. If you don't hear anything from them for a couple of weeks or so, telephone to make sure the application has arrived. At the same time offer to send more information if it would be helpful or suggest a meeting. If you know someone who knows the donor personally or professionally, you could ask her/him to make some discreet enquiries about what is happening to your appplication.

If you are applying to a local authority, both councillors and officers expect to be lobbied directly, so lobby then. Write to them, go and see them at their surgeries and collar them after committee meetings.

If you are applying to a trust, the trust secretary will expect to process all the applications, but if you know a trustee personally, by all means mention your application to her/him. Sometimes trustees are extremely active when it comes to promoting their pet projects.

With companies the best possible thing is to get someone who knows you and who also knows one or other of the company's directors to mention your work to them. You could also get a friendly businessperson to sign your appeal letter.

Lobbying will almost always promote your cause. Once your application has gone off, don't sit back and wait to be assessed solely on merit. The Old Pals' Act operates here just like everywhere else.

Keep records

On a card index you should log the following information:

- Name of donor
- Address
- Telephone number

103

- Name of correspondent (the person you write to)
- Date application sent
- Amount requested
- Date reply received
- Comments. Each donor body has its own little idiosyncracies. They may not like people to telephone them, for example. This kind of information is worth logging.

If you are a membership organisation you will need to keep records of the support you receive from individuals such as annual subscription rates, whether or not they make additional donations by standing order or covenant and when renewals are due.

Successful appeals

When you succeed you should write to thank the donor immediately and try to keep in touch with them. Many donors monitor grants closely but in any event you should always send them your annual report or accounts, or any other new publications you produce, particularly any report of the work they have funded. If conditions are attached to the grant, make sure you fulfil them. Always spend the money on the thing you said you were going to spend it on. If you can't, you must go back to the donor and discuss the problem or return the money.

Once you've begun a relationship with a donor try to get regular support from them. If they set a time limit on further applications, go back with something new when the limit expires. You should do everything you can to keep your donors happy and interested in your work.

Unsuccessful appeals

You may be told that the donor cannot support your work, or that their funds are fully allocated for the foreseeable future. When they reply refusing your request, make a note of their comments and make sure you don't reapply. It would only be a waste of time. If they don't reply, keep going back to them. Persistence really does pay off. After a few attempts they will probably tell you that you don't stand the slightest chance or they may give you a grant after all. Find out who they have given grants to and contact those groups to see how they pulled it off. Fund raising may be a competitive business, but people are usually supportive, particularly when their own fund raising has been successful.

At all times you should follow up on past successes, even if it is merely appealing to individual supporters from time to time. Don't overdo it though! But you can usually ask individuals to support you more than once. Ask them for something different next time. Offer them something in return. And when you organise fund-raising events, have a post-mortem. How could the organisation of the event have been improved? Could you have raised more money? Were your charges too low? Too high? Did you miss an opportunity? Discuss the successes and failures while they are still fresh in your mind. When it comes to organising the same event the following year you will do it all the more effectively.

PART III

LOOKING AHEAD

Consider what it would mean if among us there were now a woman motor-car manufacturer who, with a stroke of the pen, could endow the women's colleges with two or three hundred thousand pounds apiece . . . There would be no need of appeals and committees, of strawberries and cream and bazaars. And suppose that there were not merely one rich woman, but that rich women were as common as rich men. What could you not do? You could shut up your office at once. You could finance a woman's party in the House of Commons. You could run a daily newspaper committed to a conspiracy, not of silence, but of speech. You could get pensions for spinsters; those victims of the patriarchal system, whose allowance is insufficient and whose board and lodging are no longer thrown in. You could get equal pay for equal work. You could provide every mother with chloroform when her child is born; bring down the maternal death-rate from four in every thousand to none at all, perhaps. In one session you could pass Bills that now take you perhaps a hundred years of hard and continuous labour to get through the House of Commons. There seems at first sight nothing that you could not do, if you had the same capital at your disposal that your brothers have at theirs . . . Money is the only means by which we can achieve objects that are immensely desirable.

(Virginia Woolf, 1938)

8
Strategies for Change

In November 1933, Dr Elizabeth Knight was killed in a car crash. She was a member of the family which made its fortune from Knight's Castile soap and she died without making a will. The immediate consequence of Elizabeth Knight's death was the collapse of a weekly journal called *The Vote*, which had appeared regularly since 1909 until her death. It was the publication of the Women's Freedom League which had been formed as a breakaway group from the Women's Social and Political Union and which continued in existence through the 1940s and 1950s, when feminism was supposedly dead in Britain, until 1961. *The Vote* had been produced as a stylish, well-printed periodical on the strength of Dr Knight's financial support. It continued to be published after her death, but as a grubby cyclostyled news-sheet.

It is a story which can teach us many lessons, among them the dangers of over-dependence on one source of funding; and the pitfalls of not making a will. It demonstrates the generosity of some wealthy women in supporting causes they value; and the tenacity of women's organisations in the face of perpetual fund-raising problems and 'unpopularity'.

It is this tenacity, this determination to achieve 'objects which are immensely desirable', as Virginia Woolf put it in *Three*

Guineas, which will see women through this difficult period of the mid- to late 1980s. But survival is not enough. Women also want change. Women want justice and a more positive commitment from funding bodies. The exceptional contribution women's activity in the voluntary sector makes to British life deserves to be acknowledged.

THE CASE FOR WOMEN

Women's organisations widely testify to the never-ending struggle to raise adequate funds (see chapter 2). They also testify to the neglect and discrimination they often face from funding bodies. Few funders have explicit policies in support of women, despite the willingness to recognise the other special interest groups, whether environmentalists, animals or youth. Indeed, women also point to the fact that many of the special interest groups which are recognised by funding bodies are often viewed in a discriminatory light, with male interests taking precedence over female. Youth provision is a case in point. Women working with young people have found it necessary to develop 'girls' nights' in mixed youth clubs, as a remedial measure against the male domination of facilities, activities and budget allocations.

Inequalities can also creep in on the rare occasions when 'women' *is* recognised as a specific category by funders. The failure then is to see women as a homogeneous group, a view which tends to favour middle class white women, ignoring the even greater need for money that, for example, black women, working class women, lesbian women or women with disabilities have.

Women are the majority at the heart of British society but they are treated like a minority on the fringes of our national life. Women are still expected to fit in with a male-created world, whether at work or in public life. But women want to or have to lead different lives to men. Women want to be able to combine paid work and family life without the stress and impoverishment that implies in Britain today. And yet rearranging our national life to make such a way of living the easy, natural thing to do is not a priority for policy-makers or the people who wield financial power.

Ten years after the 1975 Sex Discrimination Act, the need for positive action to help women achieve true equality is only just beginning to be acknowledged beyond the ranks of the women who have campaigned for it. Many people worry about positive action, or positive discrimination, being *reverse* discrimination and being illegal. But the law recognises that saying all groups *should* be treated equally does not mean they will be. Positive words need to be backed up with positive action. The principle of positive action did in fact get legal endorsement in the Sex Discrimination Act, but the principle has not been developed into practice very widely. It is this principle which those who fund the voluntary sector need to consider.

Women's social and economic position and the lack of political will to achieve genuine improvements for women mean that women as a group have far less money, power and influence than men as a group. Nearly 50 years after Virgina Woolfe wrote *Three Guineas*, women motor-car manufacturers are still not the norm. Rich women are far fewer than rich men in number. Despite equality legislation women's weekly earnings are still only 65.8 per cent of men's. There is no Women's Party in the House of Commons; the parties there can only muster 25 women between them. There is no Ministry for Women; there is not even an all-party group on women. There is no daily newspaper committed to a conspiracy of speech about the rich and diverse reality of female life; the most popular papers are the ones which perpetuate destructive images of women as objects of men's pleasure or victim's of men's power.

Many women believe that where rate-payers' and tax-payers' money is being used to finance the voluntary sector, then projects run by and for women, who do so much for the other members of society and who themselves are rate- and tax-payers, should receive a more equitable share of funding. For all these reasons women expect, deserve and demand more than they are getting at present.

SOME PROPOSALS

The following are a limited range of proposals whose implementation would, in part, help solve the funding problems which women's voluntary organisations have identified. Many of the proposals are based on current trends. Some could be achieved with only minor changes of emphasis or direction. Others are longer term and have far-reaching implications.

These proposals have three main objectives: to increase the effectiveness of women's own resources; to increase women's direct influence over decision making, and to make funding bodies more responsive to women's needs and the needs of women's organisations.

What women can do
Women's great talent for mutual

support is a vital key to survival. This does not imply merging groups. Nor does it imply an abandonment of autonomy. But a positive commitment to a common strategy for survival will help the widest possible number of groups to survive. Discussions at conferences and in workshops, published articles and papers have demonstrated that mutual support, networking, sharing, whatever it might be called, is favoured by women.

Future strategies need to ensure that all of the many disparate groups of women, and particularly those who face double discrimination in society – black women, lesbian women, women with disabilities – are fully represented in debates and decision-making structures.

With such a motivating principle, networks could be developed on a geographical basis – throughout a district, borough or county council area – on a project basis (such as a federation of childcare projects in a particular area) or across special interest categories of women who are doubly disadvantaged. Mutual support networks could:

- *investigate* the criteria of different funding bodies, building up detailed pictures of each of them, so that projects could be matched with sources of funds
- *exchange* and *analyse* information on the successes and failures of applications to different sources of support
- *monitor* the range of women's voluntary groups and the scale of financial need
- *exchange* skills by holding resources workshops on everything from bookkeeping to public speaking to negotiating with funders
- *identify* key projects to be priorities for support, such as women's centres of all types
- *establish* central services to cut overheads, such as reprographic facilities, management and equal opportunities training, or shared premises
- *develop* joint fund-raising and promotional activities
- *campaign* and *lobby* in a united way to reduce the competition for limited funds between different groups of women, to support the groups which do not fit any of the criteria of traditional funding bodies, such as lesbians, and to make women as a whole visible to funding bodies as a special interest group
- *market* skills acquired in the voluntary sector while acting as consultants, profit-making enterprises, trainers, researchers or service providers.

What others should do

The use to which women's voluntary organisations can put the information in this book will be severely limited unless funding bodies themselves change. At present, there is little recognition by funders of the needs of women, who often work for little pay outside the home and also are responsible for all the work and care that goes on in the home. Nor do funders acknowledge the scale of women's contributions – as paid and unpaid workers – in the voluntary sector.

In the light of this, it is simply not an answer for funding bodies to say 'We do not fund women's groups because we do not fund men's', or 'If we made women a special category, it would be discrimination.' Yet this blinkered view of the realities of male and female life persists. For example, in November 1985, the London Grants Committee, set up to administer the county-wide 'Richmond' grants scheme after the abolition of the GLC, rejected proposals to set up a Women's Unit and to require that reports on grants detail the benefits they would bring to women.

To demonstrate a positive commitment to the issues raised here, all grant-aiding bodies should, at the least, develop policies which:

- specifically recognise women's special interests
- have a strong equal opportunties perspective on the needs of disadvantaged groups of women
- acknowledge the need for development work with women's groups which often lack basic resources such as professional expertise and access to meeting places

To meet these points we make the following proposals:

1. The larger grant-making bodies, whether statutory or non-statutory, should recognise the needs of women and establish an allocation for women's projects within their budgets.
2. Smaller local trusts and funds without full-time administration should make public their policies with regard to the needs of women.
3. Central umbrella-type organisations with links to non-statutory sources of support for the voluntary sector (such as councils for voluntary service, trust administrators' groups, the Trades Union Congress or chambers of commerce), should provide regular reports and advice on the financial needs of women's voluntary organisations.
4. The Equal Opportunities Commission's s. 54 grants budget should be increased massively and the criteria for what can be funded broadened.
5. The Commission for Racial Equality should develop a

policy on grant aid to women's groups and allocate adequate funds.
6. Cuts in the geographical spread of the Urban Programme should be restored and a greater emphasis be given to supporting social needs under this programme (which was established under the Local Government Grants (Social Need) Act 1969).
7. County-wide grants schemes under s. 48 of the Local Government Act 1985 should be made mandatory, with a simple majority required for allocation of grants.
8. An independent Women's Foundation should be established with initial capital endowment from central government (similar to the London Charitable Trust being set up through sale of GLC assets).
9. A clarification within charity law such that charities can undertake campaigning work in furtherance of their charitable objects without fear of being penalised.
10. Full and better use (to women's benefit) by all local authorities of local government finance under s. 137 of the Local Government Act 1972.
11. Positive action to increase women's representation on all decision-making bodies with responsibility for supporting the voluntary sector.
12. Establishment of an independent Women's Commission to report on the scale and nature of women's voluntary organisations and to make recommendations on future funding. This commission would have a wide-ranging brief but would be particularly concerned with making recommendations for the secure funding of key, independent women's services such as Women's Aid Refuges and Rape Crisis Lines. The commission would be similar to the Wolfenden Committee whose report on the future of voluntary organisations in 1978 followed a three-year investigation into the relationship between voluntary organisations and the government.

Many other issues which profoundly affect women in the voluntary sector such as rate-capping, rate support grant, care in the community or the absence of a Ministry for Women are directly related to wider government policy. This book has been written largely in response to a crisis – abolition of the metropolitan councils – precipitated by government policy. But we have also discussed the significance of more fundamental inequalities in society. These have a long history, a history matched by the vigorous and determined effort of women themselves to meet their own needs and achieve change. Women are more than equal to the struggle. But the real challenge faces the trustees, company directors, local councillors, government ministers and their advisers. They are the people who are now being urged to give due attention to the demands being voiced by women in the voluntary sector.

APPENDIX 1
SOURCES OF FURTHER INFORMATION

Useful local addresses

The council for voluntary service and rural community council in your area may be able to offer advice and information. In some areas there may be a volunteer bureau. These organisations exist solely to help and promote voluntary organisations but they have close links with government especially and if you apply for Urban Programme support your CVS will be consulted. The CVS can give direct help or provide links locally, for example, with sources of training and help with financial management, new sources of money and newsletters. CVS will also advise on timetables and tactics when you are approaching your local authority. You can find the address and telephone number in the telephone book. Or get in touch with the Councils for Voluntary Service – National Association (CVSNA), at 26 Bedford Square, London WC1B 3HU, tel. 01-636 4066.

If there is a Women's Centre or Resource Centre in your area you may find that women there will be able to advise you, especially if the centre is heavily used by different groups.

Your local district or borough council may have set up a Women's Committee or Equal Opportunities Committee with a support unit.

There are charities information bureaux in the following areas:

South Yorkshire Charity Information
  Service Trust
40 Trippett Lane
Sheffield S1 4EL
Tel. 0742-731765

West Yorkshire Charities Information
  Bureau
11 Upper York Street
Wakefield WF1 3LQ
Tel. 0924-382120

Humberside Charities Information
  Bureau
14 Market Place
Howden
Goole
Humberside DN14 7BJ
Tel. 0430-30904

Charities Information Service (Sussex)
c/o Chapel Royal
North Street
Brighton BN1 1EA
Tel. 0273-21398

Birmingham Charity Information Service
161 Corporation Street
Birmingham B4 6PT
Tel. 021-236 1264

Wiltshire Charities Information Bureau
Andil House
Court Street
Trowbridge BA14 8BR
Tel. 02214-68848

Useful national addresses

Voluntary Organisations Unit
Equal Opportunities Commission
Overseas House
Quay Street
Manchester M3 3HN
Tel. 061-833 9244
The Voluntary Organisations Unit will not only give you advice on whether or not an application to the EOC would be successful, they may also be able to suggest other possible sources of funding. From time to time the commission has worked on the problem of how women can attract more financial support, if only to soften the blow of having to disappoint so many of their own applicants.

Commission for Racial Equality
10–12 Allington Street
London SW1 5EH
Tel. 01-828 7022
The CRE with its regional offices and the Community Relations Councils at local level, may be able to help ethnic minority women. Contact the CRE at the above address.

Voluntary Services Unit
The Home Office
50 Queen Anne's Gate
London SW1H 9AT
Tel. 01-213 7079
The VSU advises on the relevant government department at which to direct applications, and may make grants itself in cases where projects do not fall within the area of responsibility of only one government department.

Community Service Volunteers
237 Pentonville Road
London N1 9NJ
Tel. 01-278 6601
Community Service Volunteers operate a scheme where they place young volunteers with you full time for a few months or longer. You are expected to provide board and lodging and pocket money.

National Council for Voluntary Organisations
26 Bedford Square
London WC1B 3HU
Tel. 01-636 4066
NCVO offers advice in a number of areas, including advice on obtaining charitable status, a VAT advice service to charities, and guidance on applications to the Manpower Service Commission and European Social Fund.

A Woman's Place
Hungerford House
Victoria Embankment
London WC2N 6PA
Tel. 01-836 6081

A Women's Place is a women's liberation information and referral service which keeps extensive files on women's activities, issues and campaigns in London, the rest of England, Scotland, Wales, Ireland and worldwide.

Books, guides and other publications

NCVO publications

SUSAN BATES (comp). *Fund Raising and Grant Aid for Voluntary Organisations*, Bedford Square Press|NCVO, winter 1986. A guide to publications on the subject.

ANN DAVISON. *Grants from Europe: How to get money and influence policy*, Bedford Square Press|NCVO, 2nd edn. 1985.

MAGGIE JONES (comp). *Government Grants: a guide for voluntary organisations* (NCVO practical guide), 3rd edn. 1986.

INF. DEPT. 'How to Apply for a Grant', Information Sheet No. 29, 1984.

INF. DEPT. 'Selective Bibliography of Fund-Raising Books and Pamphlets', Information Sheet No. 17, 1985.

A. R. LONGLEY et al. *Charity Trustees' Guide*, Bedford Square Press|NCVO, 2nd edn. 1982.

NCVO. *Equal Opportunities in Voluntary Organisations* (NCVO practical guide). Bedford Square Press|NCVO, winter 1986/87.

NCVO. *Lotteries and Gaming: Voluntary organisations and the law*, Bedford Square Press|NCVO, 3rd edn. 1983. A short guide to the law within which lotteries, raffles, etc., must be run.

ORG DEV'T DEPT. *Relations between the Voluntary Sector and Government: A code for voluntary organisations*, 1984. Gives advice on how to cope with the strings attached to government grants.

POLICY ANALYSIS UNIT. *The Management and Effectiveness of Voluntary Organisations*, 1984.

Voluntary Action published as an insert to

Appendix 1

the journal *New Society*, is on sale weekly at most newsagents.

These are only some of the publications produced by NCVO which you might find useful. For the most recent stocklist and details of prices and of how to obtain copies, write to NCVO at the address above, from whom NCVO publications are available, Bedford Square Press books are available through bookshops or by post from the distributors. Personal callers can buy books at NCVO.

Directory of Social Change publications

A Guide to the Major Trusts, 1986. Details the grant-making policies of 200 large grant-making trusts.

A Guide to Company Giving, 1984 (2nd edn available September 1986). Gives facts, figures and addresses of over 1,000 companies.

Raising Money From Government, 3rd edn 1985. Gives background information and practical guidance on central and local government giving with detailed information on grants from central and non-governmental sources.

Raising Money from Trusts, *Raising Money from Industry*, *Industrial Sponsorship and Joint Promotions* (1981). These three guides give background information and practical guidance on fund raising.

Money and Influence in Europe, 1983. Gives advice and detailed contacts for getting money from the EEC.

Raising Money by Advertising, 1986. Covers direct mail and radio and television appeals as well as poster and newspaper advertising.

Legacies: a practical guide, *Leaving Money to Charity* (1983). These are two guides to getting legacy income, the first for charities, the second for their supporters.

Covenants: a practical guide, 3rd edn 1985. A comprehensive guide to the tax advantages of giving including model forms for use by charities.

A Guide to the Benefits of Charitable Status, 1983. A complete guide to all the benefits of being a charity and how to get them.

Investment of Charity Funds, 1985. Shows how to invest your short-term cash balance and long-term reserves to get the best income.

Fund-raising Notes for Capital Projects, 1985. A set of 12 leaflets giving advice on all aspects of fund raising for those involved in a capital project.

Accounting and Financial Management for Charities, 2nd edn 1985. A basic handbook to understanding the accounts, how to keep your books and using financial information to manage your organisation.

Charities Aid Foundation publications

Directory of Grant-Making Trusts, 1985. The best information source on over 2,400 grant-making trusts.

Charity Statistics. A yearly analysis of the statistics of charitable sources of income with interesting background articles.

Charity ('for people giving, receiving and administering charitable funds') is a monthly journal with news from and about the voluntary sector.

Details of prices and availability from:

Directory of Social Change
9 Mansfield Place
London NW3 1HS
Tel. 01-794 9835

Charities Aid Foundation
48 Pembury Road
Tonbridge TN9 2JD
Tel. 0732-356323

Publications from other sources

CYSYLLTIADUR MERCHED CYMRU. *Wales Women's Directory: women's groups, organisations and businesses in Wales*, Women's Enterprise Bureau (c/o Bangor Women's Centre, Greenhouse, 1 Trevelyan Terrace, Bangor LL57 1AX, Gwynedd), 1984.

Sources of Further Information

EQUAL OPPORTUNITIES COMMISSION AND EUROPEAN COMMISSION. Both publish regular, free bulletins with news of interest to women, often relating to sources of funding and grant aid to women's groups. To obtain *Women in Europe*, write to the Commission of the European Communities, 8 Storey's Gate, London SW1P 3AT. To obtain *EOC Update*, write to the EOC at the address above (see page 116).

INTERNATIONAL WOMEN'S TRIBUNE CENTRE INC. *Ideas on Proposal Writing and Financial Technical Assistance*, International Women's Tribune Centre Inc (305 E 46th Street, New York, NY 10017, USA), 1982. This American publication is aimed primarily at Third World projects applying to United Nations-type funding bodies, but useful all the same. Gives step-by-step guidance on preparing and writing proposals. Also includes a directory of funding agencies, chiefly governmental and international, and the major foundations. Available for reference only at the Feminist Library, Hungerford House, Victoria Embankment, London WC2N 6PA, tel. 01-930 0715.

TREFOR LLOYD & ANDREAS MICHAELIDES. *How to Manage Your Money If You Have Any*, Community Accountancy Project (34 Dalston Lane, London E8 3AZ). Good, detailed publication.

ANDREW PHILLIPS. *Charitable Status – A Practical Handbook*, Inter-Action Imprint, (15 Wilkin Street, London NW5 3MG), 2nd edn 1982.

CAROLINE PINDER. *Community Start Up: how to start a community group and keep it going*, NEC Print (18 Brooklands Avenue, Cambridge CB2 2HN), 1985.

SPARE RIB. *Spare Rib Diary* (available from Spare Rib, 27 Clerkenwell Close, London EC1 0AT). Published annually, the diary contains a useful section listing many of the different women's groups to be found in the UK.

TANYA WHITTY. *How to Keep Your Accounts: a guide for women's groups*, Southwark Women's Equality Unit (c/o Southwark Women's Centre, 8 Peckham High Street, London SE15 5DY. Free with sae, 8½ x 11½"), 1985. Geared to groups which have not yet set up an accounting system.

WOMEN'S NATIONAL COMMISSION. *Women's Organisations in Great Britain 1985/86*, Women's National Commission (Great George Street, London SW1P 3AQ), 2nd edn 1985. Includes many of the nationwide women's groups you may want to contact to develop your networking.

Courses, training and conferences

Some local councils for voluntary service and in London the London Voluntary Service Council (68 Chalton Street, London NW1 1JR, tel. 01-388 0241) and InterChange (15 Wilkin Street, London NW5 3NG, tel. 01-267 9421) run courses to improve fund-raising skills.

The Directory of Social Change runs courses and seminars. The Charities Aid Foundation makes grants to meet the cost of professional advice or training that would enable the applicant charity to achieve its purposes more effectively. CAF has also held workshops on how to use the *Directory of Grant-Making Trusts* and how to approach trusts. Details from these two organisations at the addresses above.

The Equal Opportunities Commission holds conferences for voluntary organisations. These do not necessarily make fund-raising a priority for discussion but they are a useful forum to exchange ideas and opinions.

The Commission for Racial Equality has a training department which runs courses of interest to ethnic minority organisations.

Support from companies

Action Resource Centre
CAP House
Third Floor
9–12 Long Lane
London EC1A 9HD
Tel. 01-726 8987

119

Appendix 1

Specialises in providing secondments from industry particularly to assist employment projects.

Business in the Community
227a City Road
London EC1V 1LX
Tel. 01-253 3716
A business-led partnership sponsored by 130 major companies concerned with promoting local economic initiatives.

Retired Executives Action Clearing House
89 Southwark Street
London SE1 0HD
Tel. 01-928 0452

REACH provides retired executives on a full or part-time basis to help in a voluntary capacity (you pay expenses). Requests are logged until someone with the right skills who is based in your area becomes available.

Practical Action
16 Strutton Ground
London SW1P 2HP
Tel. 01-222 3341
Encourages companies to make products and equipment available to charities and employment projects.

APPENDIX 2
DETAILS FROM NCVO SURVEY ON FUNDING FOR WOMEN'S ORGANISATION

Questionnaires were completed and returned by 125 organisations, of which 46 were registered charities, 65 had paid staff and 39 were staffed by volunteers only.

£	
500–1,000	5
1,000–2,500	9
2,500–5,000	4
5,000–10,000	9
10,000–15,000	10
15,000–20,000	6
20,000–30,000	7
30,000–40,000	8
40,000–50,000	3
50,000–60,000	4
60,000–70,000	1
70,000–80,000	1
100,000 +	2
1,000,000 +	1

Q. Is work with women the main focus of your organisation?

105 groups said 'yes'; 45 added other areas of work such as:

childcare
the family
equal childcare responsibilities for both parents
campaigning on housing for women
promoting work with girls
educating the general public on sexual abuse, rape, abortion and social and domestic violence
anti-racist work
housing, legal and welfare advice
education
training
publicity

Annual budget 1983/84

97 organisations had budgets of the following amounts

£	
1–50	12
50–100	4
100–200	5
200–500	6

Sources of funding

Central Government

Department of Environment (includes 13 Urban Programmes – 75 per cent DoE, 25 per cent local authorities)	15
Department of Health and Social Security	5
Department of Education and Science	2

Quangos

Manpower Services Commission	3
Equal Opportunities Commision	1
Northern Arts	1
Reading Community Relations Council	1

Local Government

Community Chest	3
Social Services Committee	6
GLC Women's Committee	9
GLC/Inner London Education Authority	2
GLC/a London Borough	2
Housing Committee	3
Education Committee	1
Other	13

121

Appendix 2

Trusts, charities and other grant-making bodies

26 organisations received support from these sources. The average donation was between £50 and £200. Those listed were:

Allen Lane Foundation
Student Community Arts
Girls Friendly Society
Diocesan Board for Social Responsibility
National Institute of Adult Continuing Education
Karnival Appeal Fund
Northern Ireland Voluntary Fund
John Moores Foundation
Cambridge University Colleges
NHS Midwifery Budget
Local Co-operative Society
Rotary Club
BBC Children In Need
Jubilee Trust
City Lottery
Manchester Girls Institute
Jennifer Sheridan Trust
Smith's Charity
Hambland Foundation
Prince's Trust
Baron Davenport Trust
Goldsmiths' Company's Charities
Rowntree Social Services Trust

Other sources

Industry and commerce	9
Membership subscriptions	43
Trade unions	5
Donations and legacies	36
Fund-raising activities (e.g. jumble sales)	47
Sale of literature	17
Other (e.g. bank interest)	30

REFERENCES

London women's groups. Letter to women members of House of Commons and House of Lords, 1985.

F. K. Prochaska. *Women and Philanthrophy in 19th Century England*, Clarendon Press: Oxford University Press, 1980.

Andrew Rosen. *Rise Up Women*, Routledge and Kegan Paul, 1980.

Virginia Woolf, *Three Guineas*, Hogarth Press, 1938.

Index

Statutes will be found under Acts of Parliament.

Action for Benefits, *98*
Acts of Parliament:
 Child Care Act 1980, *46*
 Education Act 1944, *46*
 Equal Pay Acts, *55*
 General Rates Act 1967, *48*
 Health Service and Public Health Act 1968, *53*
 Health Services and Public Health Act 1968, *47*
 Housing Act 1985, *47*
 Local Authority Goods and Services Act 1980, *48*
 Local Government Act 1972, *46, 47, 114*
 Local Government Act 1985, *19, 21, 49, 114*
 Local Government Grants (Social Need) Act 1969, *63, 114*
 London Government Act 1948, *47*
 Lotteries and Amusements Act 1976, *82*
 National Assistance Act 1948, *47*
 National Health Service Act 1977, *47*
 Poor Law Act 1601, *11*
 Sex Discrimination Act 1975, *55, 56, 111, 112*
advertising, *82–3*
Allen Lane Foundation, *70*
appeals, *83–5*
applying for funding:
 amount to ask for, *102*
 conditions, *102*
 donors, understanding, *101*
 following up, *103–4*
 letter writing, *102*
 lobbying, *103*
 need, *101*
 presenting the case, *100–3*
 records, *103–4*
 reputation and, *101*

 timing, *103*
 unsuccessful, *104–5*
Arts Council, *27, 58*
Asian women, *92*
Asian Women's Resource Centre, *57*
Association of Carers, *53*
Association of Cinematograph and Television Technicians, *98*

Banks, *73, 85–6*
Barclays Bank, *73*
Barnet, *22*
BBC, *85*
bequests, *78, 109*
Bible societies, *12*
black women, *14–15, 20, 21, 24–5, 48, 57, 84, 110 see also* East London Black Women's Organisation
borough councils, *22, 45, 49*
Bovic, *74*
Bowman, Marion, *4*
BP, *73*
British Council, *59*
British Film Institute, *59, 64*
British Library, *59*
Bromley, *22*
Brophy, Michael, *23*

Cambridgeshire Social Services Council, *29*
Cancer Research Campaign, *16*
Capital Radio, *84*
Care in the Community, *54*
Caxton Hall, *13*
Central TV, *85*
Centre for Ethnic Minorities Health Studies, *53*

Chambers of Trade and Commerce, *96*
charitable giving, historical background, *11–13*
charities:
 incomes of top ten, *16*
 male domination of, *6*
 registering as, *25, 39–40*
 restrictions on, *40*
Charities Aid Foundation, *16, 23, 79, 118*
Charity Commissioners, *39, 40, 70, 71*
Charity Statistics, *17, 23*
childcare projects, *20*
children at risk, *63*
Children in Need, *85*
Chiswick Women's Aid, *74*
City Parochial Foundation, *50*
Cobden Trust, *40*
collections, *80–1*
Commission for Racial Equality, *28, 57–8, 113–14, 117*
Community Chest Funds, *48*
Community Programme, *60–2*
Community Projects Foundation Training Workshop Resources Unit, *63*
Community Relations Council, *93*
Community Roots Trust, *16*
Community Service Volunteers, *87*
companies, *17, 23, 41, 57, 72–6, 95–6, 119–20*
Confederation of British Industry, *96*
conference grants, *55–6*
contacts, *38–9, 74*
Co-ordinating committee, *50*
Councils for Voluntary Service – National Association, *16, 93*
Countryside Commission, *59*

Index

county councils, *45*
covenants, *78–9*
Crafts Council, *59*
Crimean War, *88*

Dalston Children's Centre, *21*
DAWN (Drugs, Alcohol, Women Nationally), *6*
day care service, *23*
Daycare Trust, *29*
Development Commission, *59*
Directory of Grant-making Trusts, *6, 71, 72*
Directory of Social Action Programmes, *86*
Directory of Social Change, *118*
district councils, *22, 45, 49*
district health authorities, *46*
Dr Barnardo's, *16*
donations, *41–2, 76–8*:
  in kind, *41*
Drug Misuse Initiative, *53*

East London Black Women's Organisation (ELBWO), *6, 26–7*
Education and Science, Department of, *54*
elderly people, *14, 47, 58, 67*
Employment, Department of, *54, 64, 67*
employment projects, *57*
engineering companies, *96*
Environment, Department of, *49, 53, 63*
Equal Opportunities Commission, *5, 42*:
  conference funding, *55–7*

grants budget, *18*:
  increase needed, *113*
grants given by, *24, 26, 27, 28*
Voluntary Organisations Unit, *15, 56, 57, 116*
equal opportunities employers, *95, 96*
ethnic minority women, *20, 21, 48, 57, 58, 63, 64, 70, 84 see also* black women
European Economic Community, *65–7*:
European Social Fund, *23, 49, 54, 65–7*
events, *42, 81–3, 84*
Ewart-Biggs, Lady, *21*

Feminist Library and Information Centre, *25–6*
fund raising:
  advertising, *82–3*
  amount needed, *34–6*
  asking for money, advice on, *42–3*
  budgets, *35, 36*
  cash donations, *41–2*
  charitable status and, *39–40, 51, 85, 86*
  collections, *80–1*
  companies, *41*
  contacts, *38–9, 74*
  costs of, *35–6*
  covenants, *78–9*
  donations, *41–2, 76–8*:
    in kind, *41*
  earning and saving money, *85–6*
  events, *42, 81–3, 84*
  importance of, *38*
  meetings and, *38*
  morale, *33–4, 44*
  non-statutory sources, *68–87*
  organising, *37–8*
  public relations and, *43–4*

record keeping, *34*
statutory funding, *41, 45–67*
strategy for, *40–1*
subscriptions, *41, 43, 77–8*
support groups, *41*
timescales, *34*
trusts, *41*
women's difficulties in, *10, 11, 17, 24, 110 see also* applying for funding

Gillick, Victoria, *90*
Girl Guides Association, *16*
GLC (Greater London Council):
  abolition of, *4, 11, 17, 19–23*
  equal opportunities policy, *20*
  funding after abolition, *21, 49–50 see also* Richmond Scheme
  grants, *18, 20, 22, 26*
  women's committee, *18, 20, 26*
Gordon, Jo, *24*
government, central:
  grants, *17, 24, 52–5*
  spending cuts, *14*
Granada Foundation, *27*
Granada TV, *85*
Greater Manchester, *50*
Greater Manchester Council, *27*
Guide to the Major Grant-Making Trusts, *71*
Gulbenkian Foundation, *70*

Handicapped children, *64*
handicapped people, *66, 70 see also preceding entry*
Hanson Trust, *73*
Hardie, James Keir, *13*

125

Index

Haringey Women's Training and Education Centre, 65–6
Health and Social Security, Department of, 29:
grants given by, 28, 53–4
Help the Aged, 16
Historic Buildings Council, 27
holiday projects, 64
Holland, 89
home helps, 23
Home Office, 54:
Voluntary Services Unit, 15, 54–5, 117
House of Commons, 12, 13 see also Acts of Parliament
Housewives' Register, 90
housing, 63
Housing Corporation, 60
Hysterectomy Support Group, 6

IBM, 73
ICI, 73
Imperial Cancer Research Fund, 16
Independent Labour Party, 13
India, 89
inflation, 35
Inner London Education Authority, 26, 46
Institute of Directors, 96
Institution for the Employment of Needlewomen, 12
Intermediate Treatment Initiative, 53
International Alliance of Women, 92
investments, 86
Italy, 89

Joint Finance, 54

Kentish Town Women's Workshop, 5
King George's Jubilee Trust, 70
Knight, Dr Elizabeth, 109

Law Centre, 93
leaflets, 79
legal centres, 58
letter writing, 102
lobbying, 103
local educational authority, 46
local government:
as customer, 48
bulk purchase, 48
cuts, 23
grants, 17, 21, 45–52
joint action, 48–9
legislation and, 46
Section 11 funding, 48
types of support, 47–9
underspending, 49
women's committees, 46
women's groups, 21
London Charitable Trust, 114
London Boroughs Grant Unit, 28, 50 see also Richmond Scheme
lotteries, 82
Lowman, Derek, 99
LVSC, 5

Manchester City Council, 27, 50
Manpower Services Commission, 17, 27, 54, 60–3
Manushi, 89
Marks & Spencer, 73, 74
Maternity Alliance, 53
meals on wheels, 23, 47

media, using, 83–5
metropolitan councils, abolition of, 11, 17, 22, 49–50, 114
Midland Bank, 73
migrant workers, 66, 67
Miners' Strike, 94
missionary societies, 12
morale, 33–4, 44
Mothers United, 90
MUKTI, 57

National Childcare Campaign, 28–9
National Council for Civil Liberties, 40
National Federation of Women's Institutes, 5–6, 14
National Society for Women's Suffrage, 13
National Trust, 16, 78
National Union of Journalists, 29
National Union of Public Employees, 29
National Union of Townswomen's Guilds, 14
Nature Conservancy Council, 59
NatWest Bank, 73
NCVO (National Council for Voluntary Organisations):
address, 117
code for independence, 102
Community Schemes Unit, 63
national survey, 23–9, 121–2
women and, 15
Women's Organisations Interest Group, 4, 15, 23, 93
networking, 88–99, 112

126

New Girls Network, *98*
Newham, *27*
newspapers, *84*, *111*
Nightingale, Florence, *88*
Northern Ireland Office, *45*, *54*
Nottinghamshire Women's Training Scheme, *65*
NSPCC, *16*

One-parent families, *53*, *64*, *67*
Opportunities for Volunteering, *29*, *53*, *62*
Oxfam, *16*

Pankhurst Trust, *27*, *80*
parish councils, *45*
Partnership Areas, *63*
'payroll giving', *99*
Peterborough City Council, *29*
Peterborough Rape Crisis Line, *29*
Pethwick-Lawrence, Emmeline and Fred, *13*
police authorities, *46*
political parties, *93–4*
poor, generosity of, *12*
poverty, *63*, *67*
pre-school children, *53*
Prochaska, F. K., *12*, *123*
Programme Areas, *63*
Project Aid, *57*
projects, budgeting for, *36–7*
public relations, *43–4*

Quango grants, *17*, *55–60*

Race relations training, *58*
racism, *58*
radio, *83*, *84*, *85*, *86*
raffles, *82*
Rape Counselling and Research Project, *53*
rape crisis services, *23*, *55*, *70*, *114*
rate capping, *23*
rate relief, *17*, *48*, *85*
refugees, *67*
Regional Arts Association, *58–9*
regional councils, *15*
Regional Tourist Boards, *59–60*
Resource Centre, *93*
Retired Executives Action Clearing-House, *86*
Richmond Scheme, *26*, *49*, *113*
Rights of Women, *6*
Royal Jubilee Trusts, *68*
Royal Masonic Institution for Girls, *16*
Royal National Lifeboat Institution, *16*
RSPCA, *78*

Sainsbury's, *74*
Salvation Army, *16*
Save the Children Fund, *16*
school, *14*
Scottish Office, *54*
Seacole, Mary, *88*, *89*
Section 11 funding, *48*
Sexual and Personal Relationships of the Disabled, *53*
Shell UK, *73*
sick people, *14*
Society of Civil and Public Servants, *98*
Soroptimists, *14*, *90*
South Glamorgan Women's Workshop, *66*
Southwark Female Society for the Relief of Sickness and Extreme Want, *12*
Spare Rib Diary, *93*
sponsorship, *73*, *82*
Sports Council, *59*, *64*
Standing Conference of Women's Organisations, *15–16*
statutory funding, *41*
Stockwell Women's Lift Service, *21*
Stramullion Co-operative, *57*
subscriptions, *43*, *77–8*
suffrage, women's, *12–13*
support groups, *41*
sweepstakes, *82*
Sylvia Pankhurst Memorial Lecture, *27*

Television, *83*, *85*, *86*
Thames Help Trust, *85*
Thames TV, *85*
Times, The, *12*
Times 1,000, *75*
tombolas, *82*
town councils, *45*
Townswomen's Guilds, *14*, *92*
Trade and Industry, Department of, *54*
Trades Councils, *95*
Trades Union Congress, *95*, *113*
Trade Union Directory: A Guide to All TUC Unions, *95*
trade unions, *28*, *93–5*, *96 see also under names of individual unions*
trade unions, women's, *12*
Traditional Urban Programme, *64*
training, *20*, *66*
Transport and General Workers Union, *98*

127

Index

trusts:
 application to, *41, 43, 72*
 GLC's abolition and, *26*
 grants, *28*
 information on, *70–1*
 ITV stations and, *85*
 objects, *69*
 operation of, *68–70*
 policies, *69*
 trustees' attitudes, *70*

Under-Fives Initiative, *53*
unemployed people, *17, 53, 62, 63, 67, 74*
Unilever, *73*
United Funds, *99*
United States, *89*
Urban Programme:
 applications, *64–5, 101*
 cuts, *23*
 grants given, *24, 27, 57, 63–5*

Vickers, Lady, *21*
voluntary organisations:
 charitable status, *39–40, 51, 85, 86*
 definition, *10*
 finance of, *16–18, 24*
 increase in number of, *15*
 management, *32*

 objectives, *33*
 see also following entry and fund raising
voluntary organisations, women's:
 changes needed, *109–15*
 history of, *11–13*
Voluntary Projects Programme, *60, 62*
Volunteer Centre, *62, 86*
volunteers, *86*
Vote, The, *109*

Welsh Office, *54*
Westminster, *22*
Widows and Advisory Trust, *53*
wills, *78, 109*
Wolfenden Committee, *114*
women:
 charitable work of, *12*
 organisations, history of, *11–13*
 power, lack of, *10*
 role of, attitudes concerning, *11*
 status in society, *10*
 suffrage, *12–13*
Women Against Sexual Harassment, *98*
Women's Aid Federation, *16*
women's aid groups, *23, 70*
women's aid refuges, *23, 41, 74, 75, 114*
women's centres, *20*

Women's Commission, need for, *114*
women's committees, *46, 93*
Women's Co-operative Guild, *13*
Women's Freedom League, *109*
Women's Gas Federation, *6*
Women's Institutes, *5–6, 14*
Women's Marches, *13*
Women's National Commission, *15, 92*
Women's Place, A, *117*
Women's Protective and Provident League, *12*
Women's Social and Political Union (WSPU), *13, 14, 109*
Woolf, Virginia, *108, 109, 111, 123*
Workers' Educational Association, *36*
workplace nursery scheme, *98*

Young Homemakers, *6*
Youth Training Scheme, *60, 62–3*

Zenith Data, *73*